Harley-Davidson EVO

Hop-Up & Rebuild Manual

Learn how to build an engine exactly like the pros

Chris Maida with R&R Cycles

Published by:
Wolfgang Publications Inc.
P.O. Box 223
Stillwater, MN 55082
www.wolfpub.com

Legals

First published in 2017 by Wolfgang Publications Inc.,
P.O. Box 223, Stillwater MN 55082

The information in this book is true and complete to the best of our knowledge. All recommendations are made without any guarantee on the part of the author or publisher, who also disclaim any liability incurred in connection with the use of this data or specific details.

We recognize that some words, model names and designations, for example, mentioned herein are the property of the trademark holder. We use them for identification purposes only. This is not an official publication.

ISBN 13: 978-1-941064-33-7

H-D EVO, Hop-Up & Rebuild Manual

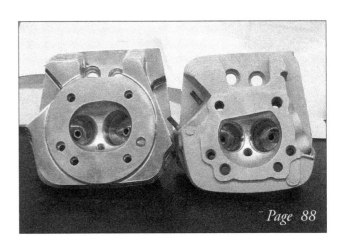

Page 70

Page 13

Page 88

About the Author

Things with engines always intrigued me. Born in the Bronx in 1953, I lived near a small patch of woods where the local teenagers would hang out and drink on the weekends. Every once in a while they would steal a car, drive it into a clearing in the woods, and strip it for parts for their hot rods. Being just a kid at the time, I would play in the car (act like I was driving) until they burned it, which would usually be a few days later. When I was seven or so, I took some of my granddad's tools and removed most of the instrument panel from one so I could still play with it even though they burned the car. That was the first time I worked on something with a motor in it.

I always had a knack for piston engines. I first started tinkering with engines and such on mini-bikes and older friends' cars. When I was 15 years old, I moved up to motorcycles. Since cash was a commodity in short supply, I bought bikes from owners who couldn't get them running. I then fixed and rode the bike until I sold it to buy a bigger one. I got my first custom when I was 17. That bike, a chopped 1958 45" flathead I bought from my older brother Larry, was also my first Harley. That was in 1971. Over the winter of 1974-75, I built my first

high-performance engine, under the watchful eye of a good friend and talented motorhead, Joe Lovallo. It was a 1968 54-cubic-inch Ironhead XLCH Sportster that I punched out to 80-cubic-inches with a set of S&S Cycle 4-5/8"-stroke flywheels and a pair of Dytch big-bore cylinders. That engine went into my first ground-up build, a rigid chopper. After working on my own and friends' bikes for a number of years, I opened a custom and high-performance shop in 1980 called CM Cycles in Mamaroneck, New York. After a successful five years, I decided to close the shop and work on airplanes. I got a job repairing piston-powered aircraft, mostly twin-engine Piper Aerostars, Beech Barons and Bonanzas, and various Cessna twins at Master Aviation in Danbury, Connecticut. After a while, I started going to college at night to be an engineer, so I could design parts for the planes I was working on. Through a strange twist of fate, I started writing technical articles at night for an airplane publication called Light Plane Maintenance. I later became its editor, as well as a contributing editor for another publication for the same publishing company called Powerboat Report. I later switched back to motorcycles and became the editor of Hot XL, a Sportster- and Buell-specific magazine, and Thunder Alley, which was all high-performance Harleys, in 1996 at TAM Communications. A year later, in 1997, I became the editor of American Iron Magazine, another TAM publication. I left TAM in early 2016 to return to aviation, though I'm still freelancing for TAM writing tech articles. I now work full time at the Fighter Factory in Virginia Beach, where I help maintain and restore vintage fighter planes and other classic aircraft for the Military Aviation Museum in Virginia Beach. I work with a very talented crew of mechanics that have been teaching me how these very-overpowered, winged beasties work.

Guess I just like things with engines, big engines!

Acknowledgements

Though I've been building high performance Harley-Davidson engines on and off since 1974, I can't take the credit for the wealth of info contained within these covers. I am mostly a compiler this time around. The engine masters that I photographed, pestered, and prodded to get this book finished are the staff (both past and present) and owners of R&R Cycles in Manchester, New Hampshire. I also need to thank Donny Petersen, formerly of Heavy Duty Cycles in Toronto, Canada, and the writer of Techline in *American Iron Magazine* since 1992. In addition to various H-D parts and service manuals I used, I also referenced *Donny's Volume III: The Evolution 1984-2000*, which is part of Donny's excellent book series *Donny's Unauthorized Technical Guide To Harley-Davidson*, 1936 To Present. They are all good friends and masters at what they do.

Reg Ronzello Jr., also known as just Reg or Jr., is one of the owners of R&R and he's the one showing you how to properly install an S&S oil pump in Chapter 2. Reg also does the wrenching in chapters 3, 4, and most of 6. As for how R&R Cycles came about, in 1993 Reg and his good friend Ray began in the basement of Reg Sr.'s house. Complete engine rebuilds, head rebuilds, big-bore kits, crankcase machine work, and mild performance work was the order of the day under the guidance of Reg Sr. Word of the quality of their work spread and by 1994 they left their other jobs and ran R&R Cycles full time. In 1995, they moved into their present building in Manchester, New Hampshire. In 1996, Ray had to leave for personal reasons and R&R became Reg Sr. and Reg Jr. By the end of 1996, R&R was developing performance packages for Evos and bought its first CNC-machining center to make custom brackets and such. But Reg Sr. had other plans. By mid-1998, they traded their small CNC for a larger one and put their first billet head into production. R&R now has five machining centers and one CNC grinder, which they use to produce engine crankcases, cylinders, heads, rocker boxes, cam covers, flywheels, shafts, rocker arms, and connecting rods. R&R builds complete billet engines from 127" to 155", as well as performance parts for the engines of other companies. It's also a full service bike shop. R&R has designed and builds what I consider an excellent line of engines that produce a tremendous amount of power and yet start easy and run smooth. The same occurs when they rework another manufacturer's engine, as I've had them do for me twice.

That said, since I won't get any glory from the info contained in this book, I'll have to settle for those royalty checks that will (hopefully) start coming in.

Introduction

There are many books currently available that tell you what components to use to make a powerful V-twin engine.

This is not one of those.

This book is about how to bake the cake, not what ingredients to put in it. If you don't build an engine the right way, at best it will not put out the power it should due to excessive internal friction. At worst, it will tear itself into a very expensive pile of doorstops and paperweights. How soon and how dramatically that happens depends on what you did wrong and how wrong you did it. This book was written to help you avoid costly mistakes and build your dream motor correctly. Most people interested in engines have heard the term blueprinting at some time in their life. This book tells you how to blueprint and assemble an Evo Big Twin engine correctly.

Back when I first started building performance engines, the art of blueprinting was spoken about with deep reverence. And yet, the bulk of blueprinting an engine is simply making sure the sizes and dimensions of the parts being assembled are within the acceptable tolerances for the type of engine you're building. In most cases, the specifications for a custom built (blueprinted) engine are a smaller tolerance than what would be acceptable in a production-built one. Blueprinting also involves making sure that all machine work is as it should be.

Once you have all the right size parts, you have to assemble them in the correct way. What I've strived to do is write the book I always found myself looking for whenever I started to work on a new machine, be it a car, boat, or motorcycle. Back in the late-1980s and early-1990s, I worked on piston-powered civilian airplanes and now work on vintage piston-powered fighter planes. In contrast, aviation manuals are very detailed while the manuals for these other machines seem to be written only as a reference for someone who already knows what the hell they're doing. That's not what I wanted to do with this book!

What you have in your hands is a reference that shows you everything you need to know to blueprint and properly assemble an Evolution-style Big Twin engine, be it a fire-breathing monster or a bone stock Harley-Davidson 80-incher. Want to know which way a collar goes in, shoulder side facing in or out? I show you that and a whole lot more. And since a picture is the best way to do that, I've got lots of them for you. In fact, just about every step is shown so you don't have to wonder what I'm talking about or what it should look like. If you are a reader of American Iron Magazine, you should be familiar with this style of tech article, since it's the same way I've done all my technical pieces in the magazine for 20 years.

As for the order in which I placed the sections, assembling an engine should be done that same way you undertake any mechanical endeavor, be it assembling, troubleshooting, or a teardown and inspection. It should progress in a logical, sequential manner. To that end, I've arranged the chapters in the order you would assemble an engine. That is, with the exception of the processes I've collected into Chapter 7: Special Procedures. Since not everyone will be doing, or will need to do, all the checks and modifications others will, this keeps each chapter uncluttered and easy to follow. And yet, I refer you to a specific procedure when it would be time to do it, if it applies to your engine build. For example, if you're building a stroker engine, you need to check the clearances of the connecting rods to the crankcases, among other things, so the stroker builder is sent from Chapter 1: The Bottom End, to Chapter 7 at the proper time. Once he's completed the necessary steps, he returns to Chapter 1 and finishes assembling the bottom end. However, the builder assembling a stock stroke engine just works his way through Chapter 1 step-by-step.

Another benefit of having each chapter cover a specific section of the engine is so someone who just wants to install a camshaft can go to Chapter 3: The Gearcase to see what he needs to do. In this way, the book is a reference manual for you no matter what you're doing to an engine, be it a complete build or just installing a new set of rocker arms.

Each chapter has a list of special tools you'll need to do the task outlined in that chapter. By special, I refer to tools not found in the usual mechanic's basic toolset. Biker's Choice, Drag Specialties, Goodson Tools and Supplies, JIMS, K&L Tool Supply, Midwest Motorcycle, Mid-USA, Northern Tool & Equipment, S&S Cycle, Zipper's Performance, and other tool suppliers offer the dial indicators, bore gauges, hole gauges, micrometers, relief tools, and other equipment you'll need. Of course, your friendly local Snap-On, Mac Tool, Sears, and other tool dealers can also help you out. A hunt on the internet should reap you more sources. And though you won't need to purchase industrial grade tools, don't buy cheap crap either. You don't want to round off the head of a bolt and then spend the next hour or two trying to get it out because of the cheap tool you used.

Many of the chapters require involved machine work. Don't try to save a few bucks by buying some half-ass tool, so you can try to do it yourself. The tolerances inside an engine are way too small to get right with shoddy equipment. There are a number of quality Harley-specific bike shops around the country that also do machine work. Some Harley-Davidson dealerships are equipped to do quality engine and machine work. You can also have a qualified machine shop do the deed. Just give them the info they need, if they are not a motorcycle-specific shop. That said, you don't have to go out and get a professional cleaning station to wash and inspect your parts. A metal bucket, long rubber gloves, and a few gallons of cleaning solvent should do the trick. Just be sure to store and use the stuff in accordance with the precautions on the solvent's container. Burning the garage down will really screw-up your build schedule. Not to mention the years of "building a hot engine" jokes you'll have to endure.

Other absolute musts are the service and parts manuals for the year and model engine you're working on. Unless you're able to pick up any part of the engine and know exactly where it goes and what year it's for, as well as every spec and installation sequence by heart, you'll need these.

So you know what you're working on and how it does its job, each chapter starts with an explanation of how that engine section operates and how the components are arranged. After all, you can't assemble an engine if you don't know its anatomy.

With over 15 years of production (1984-99), it's remarkable that Father Harley only made a few major changes to the Evolution engine along the way. If you plan on assembling a motor from a collection of parts that have never been together before in a properly running engine, you should first make sure they all can play together. You'll find what to watch out for in each engine section under the subhead Changes. I usually have a photo of one of the versions of the component in question; sometimes it's the one to avoid, sometimes the one to use. The caption below it will tell you which.

Each chapter also tells you how to prep the parts for installation, which includes inspection and tolerance checks. Some mechanics just visually inspect parts and, if no glaring defects are found, bolt the parts back together. Unfortunately, their engines sometimes come apart soon after. Don't be lazy! Check your parts, whether used or new, to make sure they are up to snuff and the proper ones for the job at hand. And, if applicable, assembly tips, tricks, and things to watch out for are also mentioned. However, you should also have on hand the manufacturer's manual and/or specifications chart for your particular engine, so you know exactly what the tolerances are for your motor. This also goes for torquing sequences, which may be different for your year and make engine.

As for the assembly photo sequences, I've used one of R&R Cycle's billet aluminum 127-cubic-inch engines as the model in most of the photos. If the assembly practices used on this torque and horsepower monster keep it running smooth and strong, they should be good for your engine, too. As for the processes and procedures, they are the same no matter what manufacturer's engine you're building, be it Harley-Davidson, JIMS, R&R Cycle, S&S Cycle, etc. However, whenever there are differences, I've included both assembly sequences in the chapter. For example, stock H-D rocker boxes are a three-piece affair, while all aftermarket vendors offer a two-piece box, so Chapter 6: The Valvetrain, has both assembly sequences.

Since you're working on an engine that was manufactured after 1979, which is when the Environmental Protection Agency (EPA) passed a no-tampering law, you cannot legally alter, in any way, a certified emissions-compliant engine and use it on the public streets and highways. Federal law requires that the engine is rebuilt using the stock cams, air cleaner, exhaust, and whatever else was required for certification for that year engine. Some states are enforcing this, and some are not. As for this book, it's about how to build an engine. Where you use the engine and how you build it is your decision.

If you find mistakes, misprints, typos, omissions, or plain ol' screw-ups in the text, please send me a message, so I can correct the oversight in the next printing. (Hopefully, there will be one.) You can do so by sending the info to the publisher of this book's web site. Believe me, I'll hear about it.

I hope you enjoy my book and find it useful. It was a real pain in the ass to do, but my hope is that it makes building your dream engine less of one for you.

See you on the road,

Chris Maida

Chapter One

The Bottom End

Where the force created during combustion is converted into the mechanical energy we call torque

CASE IN POINT

All the components of an engine have a specific purpose. In the case of the flywheel assembly, its job is to transform the up and down motion of the pistons into the twisting force engineers call torque. A reciprocating engine, like a Harley-Davidson, develops torque not horsepower. Horsepower is computed from torque using the mathematical equation Torque x 5252 x rpm = Horsepower.

This meticulously machined and assembled chunk of high-grade steel is what converts the downward motion of the pistons into the rotating force that makes our wheels go round.

Just as a complete bike build begins with the frame, the starting point for an engine is the crankcases. And that brings us to a major problem for many H-D Evolution owners. If you're planning on increasing the power output of an H-D Evo engine, make sure the stock crankcases are up to the task. Certain year cases are fine, while others can barely hold the stock, 50-horsepower engine together. The 1984-86 factory crankcases are very good, but after that the quality varied. Carefully check 1987-88 crankcases to make sure you have one of the good sets. The 1989-93 cases can be really bad. They were made from poor-quality aluminum alloy with equally poor castings. These year cases are plagued with multiple problems, including cracks, casting porosity that allows oil from the lower end to seep out of the engine, loose sprocket shaft inserts, and cylinder studs that pull out of the cylinder decks. (See Crankcase Concerns.) Another machining issue is a sprocket shaft seal hole that's too big for the seal. This permits the seal to float around in its left case well, which allows pressurized engine oil to get around the outer edges of the seal and into the primary system, or allow primary oil into the engine. Simply put, building a performance engine with substandard crankcases is a real bad idea. Be sure to check that you have one of the good sets if you're using crankcases made in any of these years. If you're rebuilding the engine to stock specs, you have a better chance of not having problems if you had no issues before. I know of several people who have over 100,000 miles on stock engines made in this year range who have not had any problems with them. Thankfully, the engine cases H-D produced from 1994 to 1999 (the last year of the Evo) are much better in material, casting, and machining quality.

If you have one of the bad crankcases, all is not lost, though you'll have to spend more to get/build the engine you want. There are two options open to you. The first is a complete engine swap-out, while the second is to just replace the crankcases. A complete new Evo-style engine from an aftermarket company will get you a set of strong crankcases, more cubic inches, a performance camshaft, better-flowing heads, and a host of other performance

SPECIAL TOOL LIST

Emery paper (200-grit)
Teflon sealant
Lapping compound (220-grit)
ThreeBond #1194 sealant
Blue Loctite
Red Loctite
Green Loctite
Scotch Brite pads
Retaining ring pliers
Electric drill
0.156" drill bit
1/8" drill bit
#31 drill bit
1-1/4" socket
1-1/2" socket
1-5/8" socket
Telescoping (hole) gauge
Flywheel truing stand
Pinion race lapping tool
Bore gauge
T-gauge
Micrometer
Timken race removal tool
Timken race installation tool
Old sprocket shaft
Flywheel fixture
Dial indicator
Bearing race driver (2)
Timken bearing removal tool
Timken bearing installation tool
Sprocket seal installation tool
Pinion bushing reamer (#HD-94805-57)
1" expansion reamer
Honing machine

enhancements not found on the stock motor. However, since you're holding a book on how to rebuild an engine, my guess is that you're more interested in Option 2: rebuilding what you have. To that end, you can buy new aftermarket crankcases from S&S Cycle, Delkron, or another manufacturer and then build the engine you want. Since you'll (hopefully) be reusing some of the stock components this may be the cheaper of the two options. The glitch with either of these choices is that the engine number will not match the bike's frame vehicle identification number (VIN). And though all Evolution-powered Harleys are registered by the frame number and not the engine number, a police officer may check to see if the engine and frame numbers match and make an issue of it. I haven't heard of this being an issue anywhere but I wanted you to be aware of it. No matter what you decide, don't try to use a set of the 1988-93 poorly manufactured crankcases to build a powerful engine. It may not stay together and you'll be right back where you started, minus a lot of cash. Sort of like a week in Las Vegas, but without the fun.

DIFFERENT STROKES

With that problem addressed, let's go over the four cycles (strokes) that a four-cycle internal combustion engine requires for one complete combustion cycle. These are called the intake, compression, power, and exhaust strokes, also known as suck, squeeze, bang, and blow. It all starts with the intake stroke. The piston begins moving downward from its Top Dead Center (TDC) point at the top of its stroke in its cylinder. At this time, the intake valve is opening, or is already open, depending on what the cam is making the valvetrain for that cylinder do. As the piston moves downward it creates a low-pressure area in the cylinder, which allows the higher (atmospheric) pressure air outside of the engine to push itself through the intake system and into the cylinder. This is because air reacts the same as water. The ocean of air in which we live exerts about 14.7 pounds of pressure on us at sea level. And just like when you're underwater, when a void or lower pressure area is created nature immediately tries to fill or equalize it. So just as water would rush in to fill the void, the air outside the cylinder does the same thing as soon as the intake valve opens. As the air moves through the intake tract it's mixed with fuel, hopefully in the proper portion, before it enters the cylinder.

Once the piston reaches its Bottom Dead Center

The H-D plastic breather gear has a bad habit of getting carbon chips embedded into its body, which then scratch and gall the breather gear well in the right crankcase as you see here.

(BDC) point of the intake stroke, it starts back up the cylinder on its compression stroke. The intake valve is usually still open, since there's so much volume over the piston at this point that the upward motion of the piston will not stop the inwardly rushing fresh air/fuel mixture. At some point, the intake valve will close, as dictated by the camshaft, and the cylinder will be sealed tight, so the piston can compress the air/fuel mixture to whatever ratio the builder has designated. As the piston gets close to TDC, it causes lots of turbulence in the cylinder, which aids in thoroughly mixing the air and fuel thanks to the squish band created by the head's combustion chamber design. That is, if the builder set the proper amount of squish when he built the engine (see Chapter 7: Special Procedures).

At a predetermined flywheel position, before the piston again reaches its TDC point, the ignition system will fire the spark plug and ignite the air/fuel mixture. This must happen before TDC since it takes time for the mixture to ignite and burn enough to create the heat, and therefore the pressure, needed to drive the piston down on its power stroke. For the combustion event to create the maximum amount of power, the burning mixture must create the most pressure when the piston is just past and still close to TDC and moving downward on the power stroke. If the plug fires too late, the piston has traveled too far down the cylinder and is speeding away from the ignition

event. Result: the maximum amount of force is not exerted on the top of the piston, so the engine's power output is lower than it should be. Ignite the mixture too soon and pressure is created while the piston is still moving up on the compression stroke. In this scenario, the engine is working against itself, with low-power output and possible severe engine damage the result.

Before the piston reaches its BDC position on the power stroke, the exhaust valve opens to allow the hot expanding exhaust gases to leave the cylinder and make room for the fresh air/fuel mixture charge needed for the next combustion cycle. At this point of the power stroke, whatever pressure is leftover from the combustion event is not strong enough to develop any more downward push on the piston. However, it can push the burnt gases out of the cylinder and into the exhaust system, which is why some cams open the exhaust valve early. As the piston passes its BDC point, the exhaust valve opens, if it is not already open.

H-D offers this new style of pinion bearing in four different sizes, which are colored coded for easy identification. This bearing pack can be used with both styles of pinion races and shafts.

11

As the piston rises on the exhaust and final stroke of the combustion cycle, it pushes the rest of the exhaust gases out of the cylinder. However, before it reaches its TDC point, the intake valve may have already started opening, depending on the cam chosen. Since the exiting exhaust gases create a low-pressure area in the cylinder, the savvy builder installs a cam that allows him to use the exiting exhaust gases to help draw in a fresh air/fuel charge. This is called scavenging. At this point, before the piston has reached its TDC point on its exhaust stroke, both the intake and exhaust valves are usually open. Once the piston hits TDC, the new combustion cycle begins. If both the intake

and exhaust valves are still open at this point, it's called valve overlap. At some point on the intake stroke, the exhaust valve does close and the process continues as previously described. And yes, I left out the fact that the exhaust valve may be open during the description of the intake stroke - to make it easier to understand the process.

The points of flywheel rotation, and, therefore, the location of the piston in its cylinder when the intake and exhaust valves open and the spark plug fires, is critical; so a method of reference was needed. Since the flywheel assembly is a circle, the four cycles of the combustion event are measured in degrees of flywheel rotation with one full rotation of the flywheel assembly being 360 degrees. It takes two strokes of the engine to make one full rotation, so each stroke is 180 degrees, one half of 360. Since two full rotations of the flywheels are needed for one complete combustion cycle, a four-cycle engine, like our beloved Milwaukee V-twins, have 720 degrees of flywheel rotation for each four-stroke combustion cycle.

Let's use a typical performance cam's specification sheet as an example of how this reference system is used. If you look at the specs for an Andrews EV51 camshaft, you'll see a couple of headings called valve timing and duration, among other things. These specs are given in degrees of crankshaft rotation. The valve timing specs are given in two columns, with the top one (28/44) for the intake valves and the bottom one (54/22) for the exhausts. The durations are 252 degrees for the intake valve and 256 for the exhaust valve. Keeping in mind what we just discussed about the four separate cycles of a four-stroke engine, here's how you would read these numbers: The intake valve opens when the piston, according to the rotation of the flywheels, is 28 degrees Before Top Dead Center (BTDC) on the exhaust stroke, or 152 degrees

This style pinion shaft was used in 1990-92 Evo Big Twin engines. It's the same length as the earlier ones used in 1984-89 engines, but this type only has one keyway and no taper.

1. The first step is to fit the bearings to the connecting rods. There are 36 short bearings and 18 long bearings in the steel cage setup we're going to use. Shown here is a full set of R&R H-beam connecting rods.

That means the exhaust valve starts opening when the piston, according to the rotation of the flywheels, has reached 54 degrees Before Bottom Dead Center (BBDC) on its power stroke, or 126 degrees into the power stroke. It stays open for its entire exhaust stroke (180 degrees). It is closed once the piston reaches 22 degrees After Top Dead Center (ATDC) on the intake stroke. (Remember

into the exhaust stroke. (Remember valve overlap?) The intake valve stays open for its entire intake stroke (180 degrees). The intake valve closes again once the piston reaches its 44-degree point, according to the rotation of the flywheels, After Bottom Dead Center (ABDC) on the compression stroke. That means the intake valve was open for 28 degrees during the exhaust stroke, all 180 degrees of its intake stroke, and 44 degrees of the compression stroke. Add them all together and you get 252 degrees, which is the duration of the intake valve, as listed in the spec sheet. Duration is how long the valve in question is actually open during one complete combustion cycle, or 720 degrees of flywheel rotation.

The exhaust valve specs are read slightly different. The spec sheet lists its timing as 54/22.

2. Start by measuring the inner diameter of the crankpin ends on both connecting rods. R&R does this on a connecting rod bore indicator. Both connecting rods should be the same size.

13

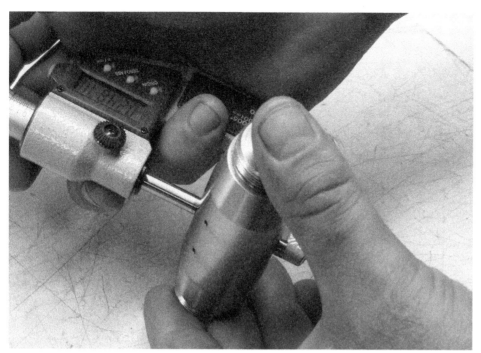

3. Measure the size of the crankpin you want to use and write down the size. The maximum difference in diameter across the crankpin should not exceed 0.0003".

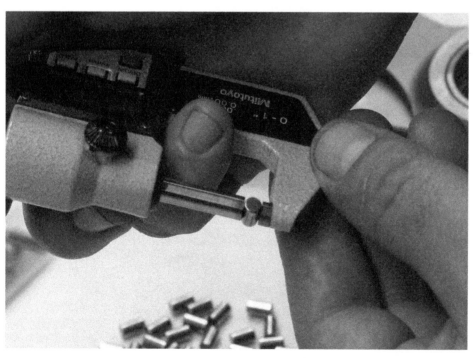

4. Next, figure out what size crankpin bearings to use. Choose a bearing size that is correct for the connecting rods.

scavenging?) Combine 54, 180, and 22 together and you get 256, which is the listed duration for this cam's exhaust.

The camshaft computations and reference points don't take into account the fact that the cylinders in a Harley-Davidson air-cooled V-twin engine are positioned 45 degrees apart. They only reference the piston's position in its cylinder since this procedure is used for all four-stroke engines regardless of cylinder positioning and engine configuration.

CHANGES

The 1984 Evos use basically the same five-piece flywheel assembly found on later model Shovelheads. This setup has a sprocket shaft and pinion shaft that are held in their respective flywheel with a large nut and a woodruff key. The single crankpin joins the two flywheels together via two large nuts, one on each end of the crankpin, and a woodruff key. The connecting rods, which connect the pistons to the flywheel assembly, spin on bearings wrapped around the crankpin. The 1985 and later Evo engines have a one-piece forging for the sprocket shaft and left flywheel, with the rest of the flywheel assembly like the 1984 engines resulting in a four-piece flywheel assembly. The late-1989 to 1999 Evo engines use a different setup: both the sprocket and pinion shafts are forged as part of their respective flywheel. These engines, therefore, use a three-part flywheel assembly consisting of two flywheels/shaft assemblies, with a single crankpin joining them together.

In 1995, with the advent of Harley-Davidson's electronic fuel injection (EFI) system, the left flywheel was fitted with notches, so the EFI system's engine control module (ECM) could read flywheel location via a magnetic flywheel sensor. (This sensor is located in the front corner of the left crankcase.) If you look at one of these EFI flywheels you'll notice that there's a single notch that's wider than the rest. This is the EFI system's reference point. By counting the notches from this point, it knows the position of the flywheels at all times, which enables it to fire the spark plugs at the proper time on the compression stroke. The notched left flywheel design was used for the remainder of the Evo years and continues today.

There are three different pinion shafts used in the Evo. The first one, used from 1984 to 1989 (#24006-83), has a tapered end for the pinion gear and two keyways with woodruff keys (#23985-54/#26348-15), one for the pinion gear and one for the oil pump drive gear

5. *If you must use a larger bearing size, but the connecting rod's inner diameter is not large enough to give you the clearance needed, hone the races out to the proper spec.*

6. *To fit the wrist pins to their bushings in the top of the connecting rods, measure the OD of the wrist pin using a micrometer.*

(#26349-73A). The oil hole for the shaft and flywheel is 90 degrees off from the woodruff key slot. This pinion shaft version also has its oil feed hole in the center of the tapered end that goes into the cam cover. It uses a left-hand thread pinion gear nut (#24023-54) and a flywheel nut (#24016-80) with woodruff key (#11218). This shaft's pinion gear uses a separate spacer (#24703-54) between it and the oil pump drive gear. This pinion shaft is the strongest of the three and the one to use in a high performance engine. The next shaft style was used on 1990-92 Evos and is part of the right flywheel. This shaft is the same length as the earlier one, but it does not have a tapered

end (see photo). It also has only one keyway, which takes a special elongated woodruff key that drives both the pinion gear and oil pump drive gear and uses a left-hand pinion gear nut. The oil pump drive gear for this style shaft has an integral spacer, not a separate one. The late-style 1993-99 pinion shaft is longer than both earlier shafts and is also part of the right flywheel. However, it, like the 1990-92 shaft, is not tapered, has a single keyway, and uses the post-1990 oil pump drive gear with integral spacer. It has a different pinion gear, one that doesn't have a counterbore on its face. It uses a right-hand threaded pinion gear nut instead of a left-hand threaded nut, like the previous two versions.

7. Then measure the bushing's ID. If the pin is too large for the bushing, hone the bushing using a honing machine or similar device. If the bushing is too large for the wrist pin, replace the bushing.

8. If you're reusing the stock flywheel assembly, check both shaft bores and the crankpin bores. Also check if the bronze thrust washers have any grooves. If they do, they must be replaced.

When H-D started using one-piece flywheel and shaft setups for both the sprocket and pinion sides in 1989, it also began using a replaceable inner race that's pressed onto the pinion shaft. This way, if the pinion race was damaged, just the race could be changed and the entire right flywheel would not need to be replaced. The measuring and race/bearing selection procedure is involved and laid out in tedious detail in any appropriate year H-D service manual. The outer race and inner race, as well as the pinion bearings, are all color-coded or otherwise marked as per their sizes. However, if one or both of the races have to be lapped or replaced, the measurement process must be carefully followed to get the right combination into the

engine. If there was a way to simplify it, I'd laid it out for you here. But since that's not the case, there's no reason to regurgitate all that info for you. Just go through the manual, follow the steps, and you'll be good to go. The process is not hard to understand, just involved.

H-D and JIMS offer the new-style (1987-99) pinion bearing pack in four different sizes that are colored coded (green, white, red, and blue) for easy identification. This new bearing pack can be used with both the old and new race setups. The difference between the smallest and the largest bearing pack is 0.0006". Harley's chart is found in any modern H-D service manual for Evos. The JIMS chart is on its web site's parts catalog. JIMS also offers six different sizes

9. To remove a thrust washer, drill a couple of 1/8" holes in the washer. Go all the way through the bronze and stop once you hit the cast steel flywheel. Make the holes about 180 degrees apart.

10. Use a center punch to tap the washer to get an edge of the washer protruding over its recess in the wheel. Then remove the washer with a pick tool. Or thread a sheet metal screw into the drilled holes to pull it out.

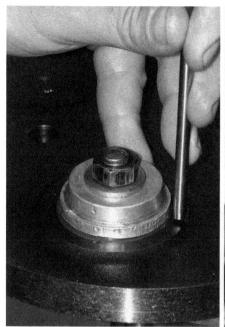  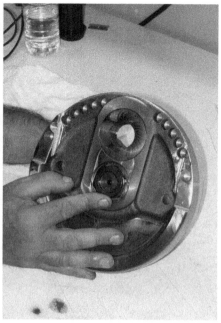

11. Using two bearing race drivers that are bolted together, press a new washer into its recess in the flywheel. Use a center punch to spike the washer in four spots.

12. To build the flywheel assembly, start by test fitting the proper woodruff key in its groove in the pinion shaft, as well as the crankpin and sprocket shaft keys and keyways.

13. Once the key is in place in the pinion shaft, insert the pinion shaft into the right flywheel so the key aligns with its slot in the flywheel. Then thread on the pinion shaft nut.

of loose bearings for the old-style 1984-86 bearing setup, which consists of a set of bearings and a cage, if you want to go that route. This is as good a place as any to let you know that many of the high quality replacement races, bearings, bushings, connecting rods, crankpins, nuts, flywheels, etc. you'll need to rebuild your engine are offered by JIMS and S&S Cycle.

PREP WORK

Before we dive into this project any further, a bit of advice: Rebuilding the flywheel assembly is not a job for someone who doesn't have the proper measuring tools or equipment, as well as the skill to pull it off. As you read through this chapter, you'll see we're dealing with extremely small tolerances and using many special pieces of equipment. That's not to say you shouldn't rebuild your own engine; that's the whole point of this book. What I am saying is the rebuilding of the heads, boring and honing the cylinders,

and assembling, truing, and balancing the flywheel assembly is best handled by a shop that does this all the time rather than a newbie to the process. That is, unless you plan on doing this often and are willing to buy the needed equipment to do the job correctly. A mechanic who's been doing everything but the lower end may, after going through this chapter, feel they are up to the challenge. If so, then you've got the right book. That said, let's move on.

One of the engine builders at R&R Cycle will assemble this section for us. Start by disassembling, cleaning, and inspecting the crankcases and all flywheel assembly components. Make sure no metal shavings (leftovers from machining), packing materials, dirt, or any other debris is in the oil passageways of the crankcases, shafts, flywheels, etc. Use a stiff bristle bottle brush, a cleaning tank, and some compressed air to clean out all passageways. Don't forget to

14. With the right flywheel in this fixture, and some green Loctite or similar threadlocker compound on the threads, tighten the nut to the proper torque for the application.

15. After doing the same with the key and keyways for the left flywheel and sprocket shaft, insert the key and shaft into the left flywheel.

16. With the left flywheel in the fixture, just like with the pinion shaft, put some green Loctite on the threads and tighten the nut to the proper torque for the application.

check all oil line fittings. While the crankcases are apart, drive out the old inner cam bearing. Never reuse an old bearing.

To remove the Timken bearing lock ring in the left crankcase, insert a pick tool through the oil hole and force one end of the lock ring out of its groove. You can then walk the rest of the lock ring out.

Check all threaded holes. Make sure they are free of debris and dirt. Crap in a threaded hole is a common cause of cracks forming in these areas. Make sure all threads are in good shape and will not strip out when you reinstall whatever goes into them at the correct torque. Now is the time to weld up, machine flat, drill, and rethread all stripped holes.

After spraying a rag with brake clean, wipe off the gasket surfaces of the crankcases, especially where they join, to remove all dirt or oily residue. Thoroughly inspect all gasket surfaces

for gouges, imprints, marks with depth, or any other imperfections that may allow oil to get past the gaskets. Pay special attention to mating areas between the crankcase halves, and the right crankcase and the oil pump.

Check the condition of the brass bushing for the oil pump drive shaft. It should not be egg-shaped or internally scored. If it is, change it. Also check the condition of the breather gear well in the right case. If the well is scoured, JIMS sells a 0.030" oversize steel breather gear and the reamer needed to clean it up, which will hopefully keep you from buying a new right crankcase. You also may be able to use an S&S reed breather setup, which I'm told works very well and may reduce oil blow-by. (More on this in Chapter 3: The Gearcase.)

Use all new woodruff keys and check the fit of the keys in their slots, on the crankpin, both flywheels, and both shafts (if used). Make sure

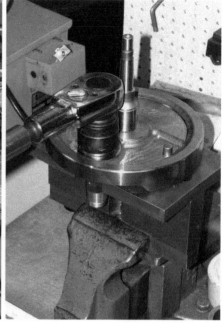

17. After fitting the proper woodruff key in the crankpin, put the pin into its tapered hole in the right flywheel with its key aligned with its slot in the flywheel.

18. To calculate connecting rod endplay, measure the length of the crankpin as it sits in the right flywheel, before you tighten it down.

19. With the right flywheel in the fixture and green Loctite on the threads, torque the nut to 180-210 ft-lbs. for a stock H-D Evo. R&R wants 350 and 500 ft-lbs. for its big engines.

the keys fit into their slot with finger pressure or just a little looser. If the key fits too tightly, sand both sides of the key with 200-grit emery paper until it slides smoothly into its keyway. Then make sure the flat side of the key protrudes up from the shaft at least 1/32" when it's fully seated in its slot. If a keyway slot in a flywheel has a burr, deburr it using a fine hand file.

If there are any pits, indents, etc., on the bearing or bushing surfaces of the pinion or sprocket shafts, replace them. If the outer surface is worn, replace the shaft. Check the threads on both ends of the shafts. Do the same for the shaft nuts (if used). Always replace the crankpin assembly, which includes the key and both nuts. If there are defects (gouges, nicks, etc.) in the tapers of the flywheels where the shafts and/or crankpin mate with the flywheels, replace them. However, if there is a ridge in the flywheels in the crankpin and shaft holes, just

remove the ridge with a fine round file. Then use a Scotch Brite pad on the taper so it's clean and smooth. Also, when reusing the stock flywheels, check the condition of the brass thrust washer, which goes against the connecting rods. If needed, replace as per the procedure outlined in the Assembly Tips section and the photos and captions.

If you intend to reuse the connecting rods, they must be checked to see if they are still straight and true. Do not attempt to straighten a bent or crooked rod; replace them. In most cases, unless you have access to a machine shop, the best bet is to replace the connecting rods with a new complete set from a reputable manufacturer. This gives you straight connecting rods with new races, bearings, crankpin, nuts, and wrist pin bushings. However, you should still check the fit of all parts before installation.

Check the fit of all the parts you plan on

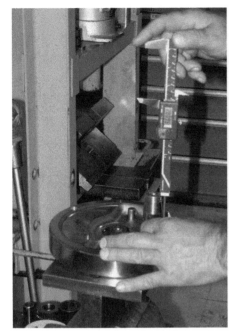  

20. Measure the length of the crankpin again now that it has been torqued. The difference between the two numbers is the crush, which is needed to calculate connecting rod endplay.

21. Check that the oil passageways are lined up by blowing compressed air through the center oil passageway in the pinion shaft and seeing if it comes out of the holes in the crankpin.

22. With the left flywheel just resting on the crankpin, use a hole or telescoping gauge to measure the gap between the flywheels.

assembling for this section of the build, whether old or new. Do this with the parts at room temperature, not cold or hot, as per the procedures outlined in the Assembly Tips section and the assembly photos and captions. As for the wrist pin's fit in its connecting rod, H-D calls for replacement of the bushing and/or pin, depending on which is at fault, if it exceeds 0.001". The same holds true for the wrist pin's fit in its piston. For H-D, the proper fit of a new pin in its connecting rod bushing is loose, 0.0003"-0.0007". On an aftermarket piston, refer to the manufacturer's specs. Personally, I see no reason to reuse an old wrist pin unless it's been in an engine for only a short time.

If the pinion race shows any signs of wear, grooves, or any other defect, it should be lapped in line with the sprocket shaft bearing race using 220-grit lapping compound. The race is correctly lapped once the entire surface has a smooth dull appearance, with no lines, grooves, or shiny spots to within 0.0003" maximum taper.

If the cam cover's pinion bushing is replaced, it should be line reamed to the right crankcase, so it will be perfectly aligned with the pinion bearing race. This ensures the pinion shaft will not be preloaded when it's supported by its bearing and bushing. Preloading the pinion shaft because of a misalignment of its bearing and bushing causes excessive wear and a loss of horsepower due to excess friction, these are two things we want to avoid in an engine. Press the new bushing into the cam cover until the top of the bushing is flush with the boss in the cam cover. Then select and center punch a dowel pin location 0.125" or more from the oil hole in the cover. Use a #31 drill bit to make a hole 0.188" deep. After cleaning away shavings, press in the bushing until its shoulder bottoms against the cover. Now continue drilling the

23. *Now measure the outside width of the female rod. Then subtract this number, plus double the crush value you got earlier in Step 20, from the width of the gap between the flywheels.*

24. *To get the endplay needed, R&R surface ground 0.010" off the female rod (0.005" off both sides of the rod). After deburring all machined parts, wash all parts in cleaning solvent, then soap and water.*

25. *After inserting a full set of short bearings into their cage (retainer), slip the bearings onto the crankpin with the open side of the cage facing up.*

dowel hole until it is 0.281" deep from the outer face of the bushing. After you clean away all shavings, sink the dowel pin into the hole you just made until it's just below the edge of the bushing, but no more than 0.020" deep. Then peen over the edges of the bushing so the dowel pin will not fall out. You can now use H-D pinion bushing reamer #HD-94805-57 to ream the cam cover pinion bushing out to the proper diameter. The tool must be sent through the pinion race in the right case and into the cam cover bushing, so the bushings are in alignment when you're done.

If needed, replace and pin the camshaft bushing in the cam cover in the same way. The cam bushing should be line-reamed to the right crankcase's inner cam bearing hole to ensure the new bushing properly lines up with the inner cam bearing. To do this, use a 1" expansion reamer to ream the cam cover bushing out to a 1.002"-1.003" diameter. This tool must be sent through the right case's inner cam bearing hole and into the cam cover bushing to keep them in alignment. However, you need to also drill a new oil hole through the new cam bushing using a 0.156" bit. The oil hole in the cam cover's bushing boss should be used as the guide for the new oil hole, since they must be aligned for oil to flow freely and lubricate the outer end of the camshaft in the cam cover.

If you're going to run a high-lift radical camshaft in this engine, you should check the gap between the inner most cam lobe and the upward curved ridge in the right crankcase. This upward curved ridge is just above the pinion bearing and just below the inner camshaft bearing. When the lower end is already assembled and you're checking the camshaft for endplay and proper fitment this check is done through one of the lifter block holes in the right crankcase using a 0.035"-thick wire. However, checking it now means not having to be con-

 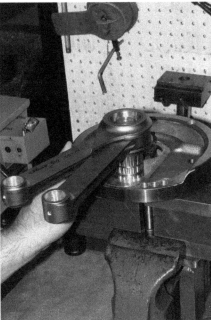 

26. *After assembling the other two bearing sets, drop these onto the crankpin, with the short bearings set with the open end facing down and against the long bearing set.*

27. *After putting the male rod inside the female (noting its offset), slip them over the crankpin bearings with the male rod positioned for the front cylinder and the female for the rear.*

28. *If you haven't put any assembly lube on the bearings yet, pre-lube the rod bearings liberally with motor oil now.*

cerned about metal shavings going places they shouldn't like into bearings or gears. Thankfully, unless you're going to use a high-lift radical cam, there's usually enough clearance here, but you should check it anyway to be sure and it's easier to do it now. Place the camshaft into its inner cam bearing and rotate the cam so its innermost cam lobe has its peak right above this ridge in the right crankcase. Make sure you have the camshaft perfectly straight in its bearing. Now pass the 0.035"-thick wire, which is the minimum clearance you want here between the peak of the cam lobe and all points along the ridge. More than 0.035" clearance is fine. If you have less, you'll need to machine the section of the right crankcase that's too close to the cam lobe to get the clearance you need. Once done, make sure there's no metal debris or shavings left in the gearcase compartment.

Assembly Tips

There are two connecting rod bearing styles that can be used in an Evo engine. One has a steel cage, while the other has an aluminum one. The steel cage setup has 36 short bearings (0.1875" x 0.325", standard size) and 18 long bearings (0.1875" x 0.660", standard size). In 1973, H-D went to an aluminum cage, which has one less roller per assembly, instead of the steel version it had been using. There are three bearing assemblies per set of connecting rods. The rollers used with the aluminum cages are not the same length as the steel ones, so do not mix them. Use the bearings made by the cage manufacturer you choose. S&S Cycle sells an assembled steel retainer and bearing roller assembly with standard and oversized crankpins, as does R&R Cycle. JIMS also sells an assembled steel retainer and bearing roller assembly with standard and oversized crankpins, as well as

23

 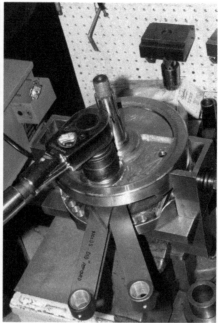 

29. The left flywheel can now be placed onto the crankpin and the crankpin nut threaded on, with some green Loctite on its threads.

30. With the flywheels in this fixture, torque the left crankpin nut to 500 ft-lbs. using a 1-1/2" socket. H-D calls for 180-210 ft-lbs. for a stock Evo.

31. Double check rod endplay using a feeler gauge between outer face of the top side of the female rod and left flywheel. R&R wants 0.020" to 0.040". H-D calls for 0.005"- 0.025" for a stock Evo.

quality steel retainers and matching bearings in a variety of sizes, and crankpins. Take the hint from these three giants in the high performance engine biz, go with the steel retainer setup, which has more bearings to carry the load. Also, do not use a stock single-hole crankpin; use a two- or three-hole crankpin. They deliver more oil to the connecting rod bearings and the bearing surface of the crankpin itself.

Start by measuring the inner diameter (ID) of the crankpin end of both connecting rods. R&R does this on a connecting rod bore indicator. The inner diameter on both connecting rods should be the same size. Write this number down. When checking the rod races, you must check the male and both sides of the female rod at two points 90 degrees to each other. Make sure all parts are room temperature when you measure them and do not hold them in your hand too long and heat them up, which may change their dimensions and screw up your

measurements. The difference in ID for the two female connecting rod races must not exceed 0.0001". The difference in ID between the races of the male and female connecting rod must not exceed 0.0002". As for each race, it must be round to within 0.00025", meaning the difference in the smallest and largest ID measurement of one rod race must be less than 0.00025". If the ID of the races are not the same or out of spec, you'll need to hone the three connecting rod races to correct the problem.

Then measure the size of the new crankpin you want to use and write down the size. Be sure to also measure the crankpin's diameter across its length. The maximum difference in diameter across the crankpin should not exceed 0.0003". If it's more than that, fail the crankpin and get another one. Never reuse an old pin.

You must now figure out what size new crankpin bearings to use. Make sure the bearings are room temperature when you measure them. As with the races and crankpin, do not hold them too long and heat them up, which may change their dimensions. Bearings come in a standard size of 3/16" (0.1875") and oversizes in 0.0002" increments for male rods and 0.0004" increments for female rods up to 0.001" over. After that, they are 0.002" and 0.003" over. Once you choose a bearing size, make sure the diameter of all the bearings you use are within 0.0001" of each other. If needed, you can also hone the connecting rod races out to get the proper clearance. Here's an example of what you may get: a 1.6265" connecting rod race diameter minus a 1.2498" crankpin diameter, minus 0.1875" for the rod bearings times two results in a clearance of 0.0017". According to the crew at R&R, a 0.0010" minimum and 0.0015" maximum clearance is the way to go on a high performance, big-inch engine. H-D calls for 0.0004"-0.0017" for a stock 80" Evo. In both instances, you are either past acceptable specs or on the outer limit. If you find that you must use a larger bearing size because there's too much clearance, as we are with this example, but the connecting rod's inner diameter is not large enough to give you the clearance you need with the next size larger bearings, have the connecting rod races honed out to the proper spec on a Sunnen honing machine or similar device. You want the clearance to be in the middle of the two extreme limits of the spec. Do not use a

32. *The flywheels can now go into the truing stand to be trued. R&R wants no more than 0.001" runout on the shafts and usually gets 0.0005". H-D calls for 0.0000"-0.0045" for a stock Evo.*

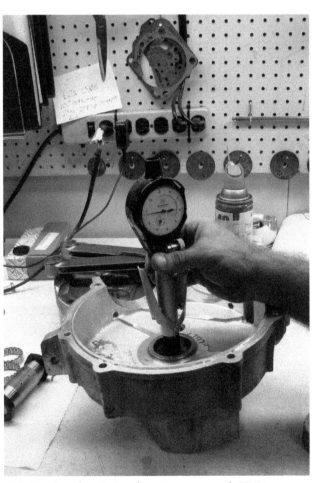

33. *Use a large plastic mallet to hit one of the flywheels to bring the assembly into true. Never hit the wheels on the truing stand. Put them into the same fixture used to torque them together.*

34. *To size the pinion bearing to a stock H-D or other right case, use a bore gauge to measure the inner diameter of the pinion race, after it has been machined with the proper lapping tool.*

35. A less sophisticated way to measuring the pinion race's inner diameter is with a T-gauge.

36. Then measure the T-gauge with a micrometer. We got 1.751" in both instances.

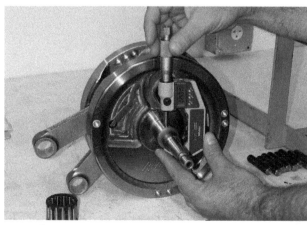

37. The next step is to measure the pinion shaft with a micrometer. We got 1.250".

lapping tool or drill-mounted honing bar. These tools are not precise enough for this job.

The next step is to fit the wrist pins to their bushings in the top of the connecting rods. First measure the outer diameter of the wrist pin using a micrometer and write this number down. The standard size is 0.9270". Then measure the ID of the connecting rod bushing using a dial bore gauge. Take the measurement in different locations in the bushing to see if it is tapered. (If it is, remove it and press in a new one.) Now subtract the wrist pin diameter from the connecting rod bushing diameter to get the clearance between the two. Ours was 0.0008", which is about right. The target is 0.0005"-0.0012". Do the same for both wrist pin bushings. You can also use a telescoping gauge to get the bushing's inner diameter, but it will not tell you if the bushing is tapered. In this instance, a dial bore gauge is best.

If you're reusing the stock flywheel assembly, check the condition of the bronze thrust washer in each flywheel. If the washer has any grooves in it, replace it. To remove the washer, drill a couple of 1/8" holes in the washer. Go all the way through the bronze and stop once you hit the cast steel flywheel. Make the holes about 180 degrees apart. Then use a center punch to tap the washer so it turns in its bore in the flywheel to get an edge of the washer to protrude over its recess in the wheel. Once you get a lip of the washer above the edge, you can remove the washer with a pick tool. Or thread a sheet metal screw into the holes you drilled and pull the washer out. Do the washer in each flywheel in the same way. Then use two bearing race drivers that are bolted together to press a new washer into its recess in each flywheel. Now use a center punch to spike the washer in four spots, all 90 degrees from each other, to hold it in place.

If you're going to balance the lower end, it must be done before you assemble it, but after you've selected all the proper size bearings, pistons, rings, etc. Check out Chapter 7: Special Procedures to see what this involves.

The crew at R&R Cycle prefers to put a flywheel assembly together dry, so they can feel how the components are fitting together. They also blow compressed air through all the oil passageways before they assemble the flywheels so they know the passageways are all clear of debris. They do the same thing once the flywheel assembly is finished to make sure all the oil passageways are properly lined up in the assembly. They then squirt oil into the oil opening in the end of the pinion shaft and make sure it comes out around the connecting rod bearings.

When it's time to install the sprocket and pinion shafts in their respective flywheels, put the flywheel in a fixture made for this procedure. Then put some green Loctite or similar threadlocker compound on the shaft's threads and torque the nut to 140-170 ft-lbs. for a stock H-D Evo. For one of R&R's 127-inchers, torque the nut to 350 ft-lbs. using a 1-1/4" socket. On R&R's 147" and 155" motors, which have a larger tapered pinion shaft, the nut gets 500 ft-lbs. S&S Cycle wants 275-300 ft-lbs. in its flywheels.

To compute the endplay for the connecting rods, measure the outside width of the female rod to see how wide it is. Then subtracts this number, plus double the crush value you got earlier (see assembly photo #20) in the assembly process (0.0011" x 2 = 0.022"), from the width of the gap between the flywheels. You want to see a minimum of 0.020" endplay for the rods, with a maximum of 0.040". However, sometimes the second crush value is almost double the first one, meaning if you get 0.011" on the first one, you'll sometimes get 0.020" on the second. To always be in the safe zone, whether it's the same crush value or double the number, aim for a final endplay of 0.030". H-D calls for

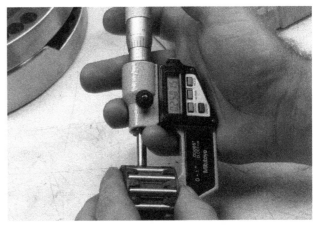

38. R&R wants between 0.0008" and 0.001" of running clearance. We need 0.2501" bearings, since 1.250" (shaft) + (0.2501" x 2) + .0008" (clearance) = 1.751" (race). As for H-D, it calls for 0.0002"-0.0009" for a stock Evo.

39. Now that the proper color bearing pack has been selected using the guide in the H-D manual, slip the pinion bearing pack onto the new pinion shaft.

40. After installing the retaining clip, R&R wants 0.010"-0.050" of endplay between the right flywheel and the bearing cage. Most aftermarket engines have at least one thrust washer; H-D just has the retaining ring.

a final endplay of 0.005"-0.025" for a stock Evo. JIMS, R&R, and S&S have their own specs.

When installing the connecting rods on the crankpin, position the male rod for the front cylinder and the female for the rear. Note: most modern male rods have an offset, which usually faces towards the rear/female rod. Check with your connecting rod manufacturer concerning any specific position requirements.

The new style of H-D pinion bearing comes in four different sizes that are colored coded for easy identification. R&R wants between 0.0008" and 0.001" of running clearance. For our instal-lation, we need one with 0.2501"-thick bearings, since 1.250" + (0.2501" x 2) + .0008" = what the race should be, 1.751". As for H-D, it calls for 0.0002"-0.0009" for a stock Evo.

When installing the Timken bearing center retaining ring, the open end of the ring must be over the race's oil hole when you're finished. The easiest way to do that is to position the gap over the hole at the start, and drive the ring in as shown in Assembly Photo 41. Caution: Once the ring is in its groove, it's almost impossible to move it without marring the case.

To set the endplay of the Timken bearings, you must choose the inner Timken spacer (shim) that will give you the endplay you want.

41. Installing the Timken bearing set starts with popping in the center retaining ring using a drift and hammer. The open end of the ring must be over the race's oil hole when you're finished.

42. Use a Timken race tool to install one of the races in the left case and keep it traveling true as it goes into the hole. One half of the tool is on the press and sits against the retaining ring just installed.

43. With the race on the case and the other half of the tool slipped over the pin that locates it to the race and case, press the race in until it sits tight against the retaining ring. Then install the other race.

 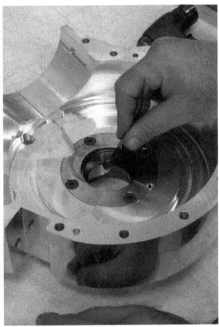 

44. *You can also use a JIMS #94547-2A tool to drive in the races. Just be careful not to slam the races against the retaining ring. You can also use this tool to remove the old races. Never reuse old races!*

45. *R&R always uses a 0.002" flat feeler gauge to make sure the races are tight against the retaining ring. If a 0.002" feeler gauge will not go in, you're good to go.*

46. *R&R uses an old sprocket shaft to check the endplay of the Timken bearings. Start by dropping on one of the two new Timken bearings.*

These shims come in 16 different thicknesses, from 0.0905"/0.0895" to 0.1205"/0.1195". To find out what shim to use, most engine shops have an old sprocket shaft that's been polished where the bearing goes so it's easy to slip the new Timken bearings on and off the shaft to check the endplay of the Timken bearings. Here's how it's done: Start by dropping on one of the two new Timken bearings. Then place the left crankcase onto the old sprocket shaft and over the new Timken bearing. Now drop in an inner Timken spacer. Then place the other Timken bearing into its race in the left case. To take up the extra room on the test sprocket shaft, position an inner spacer (start thick) over the shaft and against the bearing, followed by the sprocket shaft nut, which you torque to 200 ft-lbs. Using a dial indicator, check for the required 0.001"-0.002" of endplay. If you have too little or too much clearance, change the spacer until you have the required amount.

When installing the Timken bearing onto the sprocket shaft, put a skin coat of light lubricant on the sprocket shaft so the bearing will not go on dry. Then press the inner Timken bearing onto the sprocket shaft until it's tight against the sprocket shaft's shoulder. R&R does this in a special fixture that keeps the wheels supported during the entire process. Do not use a thick oil, since this may make the bearing stop just before the sprocket shaft's shoulder.

CRANKCASE CONCERNS

Crankcase machining and porosity problems plagued the 1987-93 Big Twins. Usually, the first indication of a problem was that the engine would lose a quart of oil between oil changes, but it isn't burning it, since the engine doesn't puff smoke and the spark plugs are clean, and it's not leaking it. So where did it go? Look in the sealed primary system. Drain the primary and see if that's where the extra oil has

47. *Then place the left case onto the old sprocket shaft and over the new Timken bearing. Now drop in an inner Timken spacer to see if this size will give you the endplay you want.*

48. *Place the other Timken bearing into its race in the left case. Then position a thick spacer over the shaft and against the bearing, followed by the sprocket shaft nut, which you torque to 200 ft-lbs.*

49. *Using a dial indicator, check for 0.001"-0.002" of endplay. If you have too little or too much clearance, change the size of the spacer until you have the required amount.*

gone. This system should have about 30 ounces or so in it. If you have a lot more than that, here's how to tell where the leak is. Remove the engine sprocket and alternator rotor. You should now be looking at the other half of the alternator (the stator) and sprocket shaft oil seal. Seal off all the engine's oil lines using clamps, so the engine is sealed tight. Then use a small hand pump, like a bicycle pump, and attach it to the engine's vent line. Pump the pressure in the engine up to about 10-12 pounds, but no higher. Then look at the sprocket shaft area on the left crankcase to see if oil is leaking out past the oil seal, nylon alternator stator wire block holddown screws, the alternator stator screws, or if the crankcase itself is porous and seeping oil. You may have to use a propane torch to heat up the crankcases to see porosity. Heat up various areas of the crankcases with the torch to simulate when the engine is at operating tempera-

ture. One area to check for porosity on the right crankcase is the hump above and to the left of the oil pump. If the case is porous, it must be replaced. If oil is leaking out past the nylon alternator stator wire block holddown screws or the alternator stator screws, the fix is to put some pipe sealant on the screw threads.

Is the sprocket shaft oil seal installed correctly? The garter spring surrounding the seal lip should be facing out towards you, it should be visible. If the seal is in correctly, try replacing it. If oil still leaks out around the outer edge of the seal, the left case has been machined poorly and must be replaced.

Another big problem with these late-1980s H-D cases is that the sprocket shaft insert, the one that's cast into the left case, comes loose. This is the steel sleeve that the Timken bearing races are pressed into on earlier Evos, all Shovelhead, and 1955 and later Panhead

50. *With a thin coat of light lubricant on the sprocket shaft, press the inner Timken bearing onto the sprocket shaft until it's tight against the sprocket shaft's shoulder.*

51. *The correct inner spacer, the one that results in 0.001"-0.002" of endplay with the new bearings installed, is then slipped onto the sprocket shaft.*

52. *After you put a skin coat of a light lubricant on the sprocket shaft and position the left case onto the flywheel assembly, slip the outer Timken bearing onto the sprocket shaft.*

engines. On the earlier Evo cases, Harley used an insert with coarse splines around its outer surface, which made a strong bond with the aluminum poured around it. In the late 1980s, this was changed to an insert with a finer spline pattern, but this setup does not bond well with its aluminum host. As the crankcases get older, the insert breaks loose and oil leaks out around the outer edge of the insert. There's no way to repair this, since it is part of the left crankcase's casting. The left crankcase must be replaced.

During 1990, H-D stopped using the steel sprocket shaft insert altogether, which means on late-1990 and all following Evo cases the steel Timken bearing races are pressed directly into the left aluminum crankcase. This is not the way to go on a very high horsepower engine, but it should be fine for anything but large cubic inch builds.

Another common problem is cracks in the right crankcase. This usually happens at the oil breather cavity above and near the oil pump. However, sometimes this crack can extend to the rear cylinder base. Once in a while, it can continue all the way to the front cylinder base by the lifter blocks. A crack in the right crankcase is also known to occur behind the rear lifter block. Cracks can be welded, but it must be done by someone experienced with aluminum crankcases, since warping due to excess heat is a major concern.

Pre-1994 Evo crankcases, due to the low quality of the aluminum castings, are also prone to cylinder stud problems. If one or more cylinder studs become loose in the crankcase it causes an oil leak at the cylinder base, the head gasket starts to leak, and the engine loses power. After a while, the head gasket will blow. One fix is to install a Ram Jett Heavy Duty Studs And Repair

Kit. The other is to weld the damaged cylinder stud hole closed, remachine the gasket surface perfectly flat, drill and tap a new cylinder stud hole, and install a new stud. (Never reuse an old stud.) Both fixes are not a job for an amateur. The stud must be perfectly perpendicular to the crankcase's gasket surface when done.

FINDING THE BUILD DATE

Want to know the exact day your Evolution engine was built at the factory? This info can be very helpful if you're trying to figure out what version pinion gear, flywheel assembly components, etc. was used in the engine. All you have to do is find the engine's 10-digit crankcase number, which is not the same as its Vehicle Identification Number (VIN). On a Big Twin, this number is located on the left crankcase just in front of the primary covers, just above where the lower of the two front inner primary cover bolts go into the left case.

Let's say our engine's build number is 1591113031. Here's what the numbers mean: The first 2 digits (15) mean the engine is a 49-state engine, while the number 20 designates it as a California one. The next two numbers (91) are the model year, as in 1991. The next three digits are the day in 1991 the engine was built. For our 1991 engine, the next three numbers are 113, so we have to count off 113 days starting with January 1. Since January has 31 days,

53. Press the outer Timken bearing onto the sprocket shaft using the same tool you used for the inner Timken bearing. The bearing is fully seated in its race when the tool stiffens up.

55. After the spacer/seal assembly is slipped over the sprocket shaft, use the same tool, but with a pusher attachment on the end, to press the spacer/seal assembly into the left engine case. INSET 54. Place engine sprocket shaft spacer into new sprocket shaft seal with spacer's lip side against the open spring side of the seal.

February in 1991 had 28 days, and March had 31, that totals 90 days. Adding the remaining 23 days brings us to April 23, 1991, which, if you check a calendar, happened to be a Tuesday. The last three digits (031) is that day's production number for the engine, meaning it was the 31st engine built on Tuesday, April 23, 1991.

TORQUING THE CASES

The H-D procedure for torquing the crankcase sections together should be followed so the crankcases are not warped and a good seal between the case halves is achieved. After putting some blue Loctite or other threadlocker compound on the bolt threads, install the bolts into the crankcase finger tight. Then tighten the bolts to 10 ft-lbs. in this order, while looking at the left side of the engine: lower right corner (5 o'clock), stud between the cylinders (12 o'clock), lower left corner (7 o'clock), top right corner (2 o'clock), left side (9 o'clock), right side (2 o'clock), upper left corner (10 o'clock), and right side (3 o'clock).

Once the cylinders and heads have been installed, torque the crankcase bolts to 15-17 ft-lbs. in the same order. Many mechanics follow this pattern, but do the second torque sequence right after the first one. It's better to do the second torque sequence after installing the cylinders and heads.

56. With assembly lube on the pinion race and bearings, and some ThreeBond #1194 sealant on the mating surfaces of the cases, slip the right case over the pinion bearing and lay it against the left case.

57. Install all the case bolts, with a little blue Loctite on their threads. Torque the bolts to 10 ft-lbs. as per the H-D procedure for now. After the top end is installed, torque them to 18-20 ft-lbs.

Chapter Two

The Oil Pump

An easy-to-install but critical engine component

Of all the major components you'll be assembling for your engine, this is one you have to get 100-percent correct! If you make a bad mistake with a piston ring, you ruined that cylinder and piston, but the rest of the engine is probably still okay. Blow it with a valve and you'll need to redo the head and maybe the piston. Screw up the oil pump and you're really going to hate what happens to your freshly rebuilt engine.

Okay, now that I've got your attention, the

This is an S&S Cycle polished billet aluminum high volume, high pressure (HVHP) oil pump kit, which is what we're installing in this chapter. However, the procedure is the same for a stock H-D or JIMS pump. (Photo courtesy of S&S Cycle)

oil pump is also probably one of the engine's easiest major components to assemble and install. That is, except for the retaining (snap) ring that keeps the oil pump drive gear on the oil pump drive shaft, but I'll tell you how to deal with that little bastard later. Before we dive into the actual build, we should go over the basics of a Harley-Davidson Big Twin Evo oiling system. If you're building an aftermarket engine, as we are for this book, the system is probably the same or similar. However, you should check with the engine manufacturer just the same.

There are two types of oiling systems used in piston-powered motor vehicles. One is a wet sump and the other is a dry sump. A wet sump is what you have in most car engines. With this setup, the oil pump sits in its supply (pool) of oil in the lowest part of the engine, the oil pan or sump. On a dry sump system, which is what's on your Evo-style Big Twin, the oil pump is not in a pool of oil, ergo the dry designation. The oil supply on an Evo Big Twin is the oil tank on Softails or the oil pan under the transmission on Dynas and Touring models. Either way, the oil tank/pan is located away from the oil pump.

The oil pump on a Big Twin engine is really two pumps in one. This externally-mounted pump contains both the feed pump and the scavenger pump in one body. Once the engine fires off, the feed (outer) half of the pump, which has the narrower set of gears (#26315-68A; 26317-68A#), draws oil from the oil tank/pan and sends it, under pressure, throughout the engine. Once the pump starts spinning, it builds up about 3 psi of pressure, lifting the pump's 3/8" steel check valve ball (#8866) in spite of the check valve spring's (#26262-80) pressure, which sends oil through a passageway in the right crankcase and into the tappet (lifter) oil screen (#24981-70). This check valve also keeps the oil tank on a Softail from draining into the engine when the motor is not running, since the oil tank is located higher than the engine. Another passageway in the right crankcase directs oil to the oil pressure

switch, which will turn off the oil indicator light once the pump's pressure reaches about 5 psi.

After the oil passes the tappet oil screen, which you should clean every other time you change the oil filter, it travels to both lifter blocks and the four (two per lifter block) hydraulic lifters. Once the oil lubricates the lifters, lifter block bores, and the lower end of all four pushrods, it pumps up the lifters and then travels up a passageway in the center of each pushrod and into the four rocker arms. Once in the rocker arms, the oil lubricates everything in the rocker boxes, namely the rocker arms and their shafts, the valve stems and their guides, and the upper ends of the pushrods.

SPECIAL TOOL LIST

Compressed air supply
Emery paper (200-grit)
Steel straightedge
Teflon sealant
Blue Loctite

The Evo early-style oil pump (#26190-73) is actually a carry-over from the Shovelhead and was in use from 1973 to 1991.

Now that the oil has reached the top end of the engine, the pressure at the pump increases and opens the pump's oil pressure regulating slide valve (#26400-82) located in the tower on top of the oil pump's body. Oil is then allowed to travel out of the pump, through another passageway in the right crankcase, and into the cam (gearcase) cover. Once in the cover, it's directed into the pinion shaft bushing (#25582-73) and onto the outer surface of the end of the pinion shaft, lubing the shaft and its bushing in the process. Oil is then sent through the center of the pinion shaft, through a passageway in the right flywheel, and into the crankpin and the lower bearings on both connecting rods. Once the top and bottom end of the engine are receiving oil at a predetermined

pressure, the pump's oil pressure regulating valve opens a little more and allows any excess oil to circle back to the feed gears and reenter the feed system. There's also a separate passageway that goes from the top of the oil pressure regulating valve, through the right crankcase and into the gearcase, so oil will not get trapped above the valve and keep it from lifting when it should.

After the oil has done its job of lubricating, cooling, and protecting the engine's internal components, it drains into the flywheel compartment. Oil from the rocker boxes drains back into the flywheel compartment via passageways in the heads, cylinders, and crankcases. Once there, the oil pools at the bottom of the flywheel compartment, so it can be picked up by the outer edges of the spinning flywheels and thrown around the flywheel compartment to lubricate the underside of

The 1992-99 pump (#26068-92) has almost the same bolt pattern as early pump, but they can't be swapped. Note fitting at the very bottom for forward-mounted oil filter used on 1992-99 Evos. Inset: Late-style ('90 and up) Evo drive gear. Spacer between pinion gear and oil pump drive gear is part of oil pump drive gear.

1. Disassemble and thoroughly clean the oil pump body and cover using a stiff bristle bottle brush. Reg doesn't always use gloves, but it's a good idea to do so.

both pistons, both cylinder walls, both upper connecting rod bushings, both wrist pins, both sprocket shaft bearings, the sprocket shaft, the pinion shaft, and the pinion bearing.

The rapidly descending pistons, one on its power stroke and the other on its intake stroke, create positive pressure in the flywheel compartment. This pressure forces the return oil from the flywheel compartment through the breather gear, which is timed to open when the pistons descend, and into the gearcase compartment. Oil from the lifters and pinion shaft also pools at the bottom of the gearcase. The scavenger (return) side of the oil pump, which has the two wider gears (#26315-68A; #26317-68A), picks up the oil that also collects in the bottom of the gearcase via a passageway in the right crankcase. Once in the return

side of the pump, the oil is sent out of the pump and through the oil filter, through the oil cooler (if you have one, which is a good idea), and back to the oil tank/pan. (We'll cover the breather system in Chapter 3: The Gearcase and Chapter 5: The Heads.) By the way, the gearcase compartment is also vented to the oil tank/pan via a fitting in the right crankcase, so the pressure is equalized in both.

An Evo engine's oil pressure should be 12-35 psi at 2000 rpm once the engine is at operating temperature. You can measure the oil pressure at the same port as the stock oil pressure switch (1/8" pipe thread), which is located in the center of the oil pump cover or at the top of the right crankcase's rear corner, aft of the rear lifter block.

The outer fitting on top of a stock H-D oil

2. Use the new gaskets to check that all oil passages in the pump cover line up with their counterparts on the pump body. Do the same for the oil passages on the pump body and right crankcase.

3. Use a flat feeler gauge and a steel straightedge to check gear protrusion from the face of the oil pump. Do both gears on both sides of the pump. All the gears should protrude 0.003"- 0.004".

pump is for the feed line from the oil tank/pan. The fitting right next to it and closer to the engine cases is for the return line to the oil tank/pan.

TROUBLESHOOTING TIPS

Thankfully, oil pumps are low maintenance creatures, unlike some girlfriends and wives. They (oil pumps) will happily keep chugging away at their appointed tasks, sending oil throughout the engine and then returning it to the oil reservoir without a need for anything other than a fresh supply of clean oil. However, once in a while a problem may come up and it's usually caused by something getting jammed between the gears. If something like a chip of metal, which is not a good thing to have circulating around inside the engine anyway, gets jammed in the pump gears the small key that keeps the gears spinning with the pump's drive shaft will shear. (That's what it's supposed to do, by the way.) What the pump stops doing for you tells you which set of gears has been jammed. If it's the feed side, no oil is getting pumped though the engine and the oil light will come on. However, if you're not the

attentive type that will notice a change in the way the engine sounds or you don't have a light or gauge to tell you something just went very wrong, the engine will tears its guts to shreds. Then it'll stop running.

If the scavenger gears stop, the pump is no longer returning oil to the tank/pan. The engine will overfill with oil and start spitting it out of every possible opening, such as the crankcase/head breathers (depending on which system you have), exhaust pipes, weak seals, pushrod tubes, etc. The good news with this scenario is that the engine is not trashed like when the feed side goes out, since the problem is too much oil not a lack of it.

It's also possible for the entire pump to stop working due to a sheared oil pump drive gear key. This can happen if a lifter's roller is starting to come apart and one of its roller bearings falls out and jams the gear. As when the feed side stops working, if you don't catch this one real quick, the motor quickly turns its moving parts into expensive garbage.

On rare occasions in cold weather, moisture in the cold oil can become slush and block a passageway in the engine or pump and cause any of the aforementioned oil problems.

Another possible pump problem is a bad check valve that allows the oil tank on a Softail to drain into the lower end of the engine, overfilling it with oil. This usually happens when the motor has not been run in a while. The culprit is either a bad check valve seat or ball. You'll know this has occurred because once the engine starts all the excess oil in

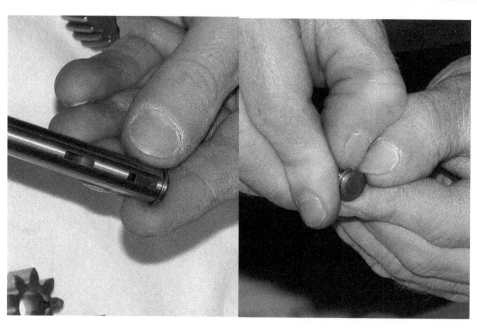

4. Install a woodruff key into its slot in the oil pump drive shaft, with curved end in the groove. Key's flat side should protrude from shaft about 1/32".
5. Install a new retaining ring into the groove in the end of the pump drive shaft. This retaining ring goes into the end of the shaft with the woodruff key slot (keyway) that doesn't extend to the end of the shaft.

the lower end will go back into the oil tank but some may come spewing out of the motor in various spots. For this reason, never top off the oil tank/pan before running the engine for at least a minute to return any oil in the lower end back to its tank/pan.

If your pump is working fine, but the lifters are getting a little noisy, check the tappet oil screen. Make sure it's clean and able to freely pass oil through itself. As stated earlier, you should be checking and cleaning this screen at every other oil and filter change. Problem is, most people don't ever service it and the lifters pay the price.

The late-style 1992-99 Evo oil pumps have almost the same bolt pattern as the early-style pump. There's one bolt hole that's a half-hole out of alignment with the earlier style. However, they look like they'll fit, which has lead some mechanics to believe they can retrofit it onto the earlier Evo engines or a Shovelhead. Not so. The pump's oil holes are also a little out of alignment with the right crankcase oil holes. If you do manage to get it to fit, oil flow will be restricted and engine damage usually occurs. This pump has a fitting at the very bottom, which is for the forward-mounted oil filter used on 1992-99 Evos.

In the assembly sequence we install an early-style (pre-1990) oil pump drive gear. Earlier in this chapter we showed you a late-style (1990 and later) Evo drive gear, which has the spacer between the pinion gear and oil pump drive gear as part of the oil pump drive gear. On the 1990 and later setup, the pinion gear and oil pump drive gear share a single keyway.

This late version is the weaker of the two options. Most high performance builds use the pre-1990 two-key design, which is stronger and the better way to go if you're using performance valve springs.

Doing the installation for us is Reg Jr., the owner of R&R Cycle. The oil pump he's installing is one of S&S Cycle's billet aluminum beauties. JIMS USA also makes an excellent oil pump for Evos.

PREP WORK

Start by disassembling, cleaning, and inspecting the oil pump body and cover. Many builders skip this phase if they just got a new pump from a reputable manufacturer. However, the safer way is to disassemble the pump and make sure no metal shavings (leftovers from machining), packing materials, dirt, or any other debris is in the pump. And since the pump is apart, why not also check clearances, like gear protrusion from the pump body, to make sure everything is on the money? That's the blueprinter's way.

Check that all passageways are clean and clear

6. Slip the feed drive gear, the one with the recessed face and key slot, over the other end of the shaft (recessed end facing the retaining ring). Then push the gear over the key and against the ring.

of debris. Use a stiff bristle bottle brush, a cleaning tank, and some compressed air to clean out all passageways. Don't forget to also check all oil line fittings. And though they're not part of the engine, be sure to clean out all metal oil lines (if any are installed) and the oil tank/pan. Make sure there's no debris or dirt from the old engine in the metal lines and tank/pan that would contaminate and damage your new engine. Install new rubber or stainless-steel braided oil lines, which have rubber lines inside. Yours wouldn't be the first motor to get chewed up by the metal remains of the previous engine. And wouldn't that suck?

If you're planning on rebuilding/reusing an old pump, thoroughly inspect all gasket surfaces for gouges, imprints, marks with depth, or any other imperfections that may allow oil to get past the gaskets. A mark with depth is any imperfection you can feel when you pass your fingernail over it. Also check both the feed and scavenger gears to make sure there are none of those imperfections on their teeth. Pay special attention to mating areas between the gears and pump body.

To work properly, an oil pump must keep extremely tight clearances between the gears and pump body. If your pump body has any damage at all, replace the entire pump. The same goes for the seats of the check valve and oil pressure regulating valve. If there's any pitting, indents, etc., replace the pump. Remember, if the pump goes out on you, it could trash the entire engine, so don't cheap out on this component. In my opinion, if the engine is tired to the point of needing a rebuild, the pump is also tired and should be replaced with a new one. If you're rebuilding the pump, install a new seal in the pump body and new guts in the check valve and pressure regulating valve at the minimum. However, you should check all clearances listed by the pump manufacturer and ensure the parts, both new and old, all fit together within the proper clearance and within spec.

Use all new woodruff keys and check the fit of the keys in their slots, both on the shafts and in the gears. Make sure the keys fit into their slot with finger pressure or just a little looser. If the key fits too tightly, sand both sides of the key with 200-grit emery paper until it slides smoothly into its keyway. Then make sure the flat side of the key protrudes up from the shaft at least 1/32" when it's fully seated in its slot.

After spraying a rag with brake clean, wipe off the inner face of the pump body, as well as the case where the pump will go, to remove all dirt or oily residue.

Check that the oil passages on the pump cover line up with the ones on the pump body. Do the

7. Put some assembly lube on the inner face and outer edges of the oil pump's inner seal. Also put some lube on both of the stationary shafts in the pump body.

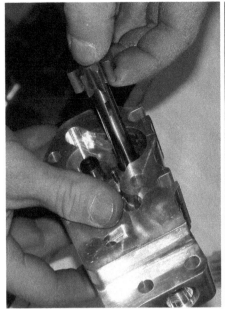 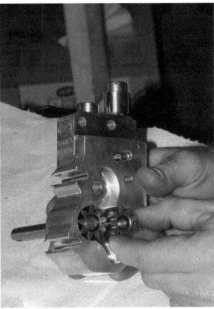 

8. Carefully slip the drive shaft into the front (outer face) of the oil pump body. Push the shaft in until the drive gear is in the pump body.

9. With the oil pump drive shaft and feed drive gear fully installed into the pump body, slip the non-keyed feed idler gear onto the pump's stationary shaft.

10. Carefully turn the oil pump around, using a needlenose pliers, install inner woodruff key into its slot in oil pump drive shaft. Do not put a mark on the key with the pliers.

same for the passages on the pump body in regard to the crankcase. Do this by laying the new gaskets against the parts in question and then the crankcase. If the holes in the part/case line up perfectly with the holes in the gasket, you're good to go. This also checks that the gaskets are the correct ones for the build. If there's a discrepancy, determine if the pump is at fault, or just the gasket kit. Remember, there's one bolt hole on the late-style 1992-99 Evo oil pumps that's a half-hole out of alignment with the earlier style pumps. If you mistakenly use the wrong pump gaskets and/or parts and get them to fit, oil flow will be restricted and engine damage usually occurs.

Also check the gear protrusion from the face of pump. You'll need a flat feeler gauge and a steel straightedge for this. Check both feed gears and both scavenger gears of the pump. The feed gears, which are narrower than the two scavenger gears, should protrude 0.003"- 0.004" beyond the face of the pump body when in their positions in the pump. The scavenger gears are the wider gears

and they should protrude from their location in the oil pump body the same amount.

Lastly, make sure the opening of the snap ring that keeps the oil pump drive gear on the oil pump drive shaft -- it resides on the inner end of the oil pump drive shaft in the gearcase -- is smaller than the width of the key slot in the shaft when the ring is installed on the shaft. If it's not, the key could work its way out of the shaft and gear during engine operation, immediately stopping the oil pump and the flow of oil through the engine. The engine itself will stop a short time later. You also do not want the gap in the retaining ring to be next to the key once the retaining ring is installed. Position the retaining ring's gap 180 degrees away from the keyway.

You may want to have a couple of these retaining rings on hand in case you overextend one while trying to get it on the shaft. The retaining ring must fit snugly to the shaft, or it will pop off. Test fit it to the shaft before you install the shaft to see the width of the opening as compared to the keyway. You also want to see how the retaining ring fits in its groove when properly installed and not deformed. This way you'll know how it's supposed to be later on during assembly.

Having said all that, if you are a novice at the ways of the retaining ring, I suggest you practice a bit before doing the deed for real. Here's how: first buy about five of the suckers, which should cost you all of about five bucks or so. Second, plug the center of the inner cam bearing with a rubber cork or something else that will not leave particles in the bearing. This is so nothing, like a popping retaining clip, can get though the bearing and into the flywheel assembly. Sure, there's not much chance of that happening, but if it does you could spend the next half-hour or half-day trying to get it out. Or worst yet, it may go in

there, but you don't know it because you think the errant clip fell on the floor somewhere. A stupid mistake like this can trash your motor at any point in the future, usually at the most inopportune time.

With the prep work done, slip just the oil pump drive shaft though the right crankcase and have the end protrude into the gearcase the same as it would if the oil pump was attached to it (see photo 15). Then slip the oil pump drive gear onto the end of the gear drive shaft without the woodruff key in the shaft. Then practice installing the retaining ring into its groove in the drive shaft using a snap ring pliers and your finger, as shown in photo 16. Finesse and skill will get the job done here. Forcing the ring on will only deform it. If the fit of the ring in its groove is sloppy, you

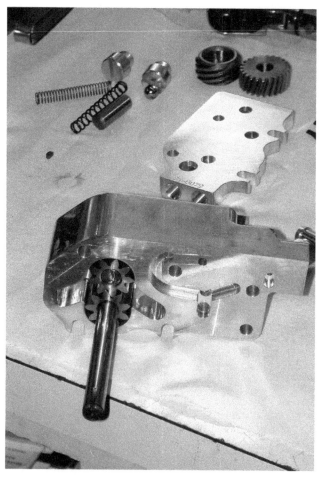

11. Gently push the scavenger drive gear over the key and into its place inside the oil pump body.

12. The non-keyed scavenger idler gear is the last one in. Slip it over its stationary shaft and into its place inside the body of the pump. Then clean the oil pump body and crankcase interfaces.

have overextended it and it cannot be used. Try different ways to position the tool and/or your finger to get the retaining ring onto the end of the shaft so the retaining ring is fully in its groove and fits snugly to the end of the shaft. The best way is to be able to do it with just your finger. Once you've got this skill mastered, you're ready to assemble the oil pump and properly install it.

ASSEMBLY TIPS

Start by disassembling and thoroughly cleaning the oil pump body and cover using a stiff bristle bottle brush. Check that all passageways in the oil pump body and cover are clear and clean of dirt, metal shavings, or packing material. Also check all oil-line fittings.

When installing the feed drive gear (the two feed gears are narrower than the scavenger gears)

with the recessed face and key slot, slip it over the end of the drive shaft without the retaining ring so the recessed end of the gear faces the retaining ring you already installed. Then push the feed drive gear all the way over the shaft, over and engaging the key, and against the retaining ring. When properly positioned, the retaining ring should fit cleanly in the recess in the face of the feed gear.

To install the drive shaft into the front (outer face) of the oil pump body, put some oil on the drive shaft and seal. Then gently move the shaft from side to side to work it into the seal. Just shoving the shaft through the seal will probably make the key slot on the end of the shaft cut a small chunk out of the seal. Not good!

When putting the scavenger drive gear, the

13. *Squirt some engine oil (not assembly lube) into the crankcase's drive shaft bushing. Then wipe away any excess oil that drips from the bushing onto the crankcase-oil pump gasket surface.*

14. *After putting a new pump gasket on the crankcase, install the oil pump's drive shaft through the crankcase bushing and position the oil pump against the crankcase.*

one with the keyway, onto the drive shaft, gently push it over the key (don't knock the key out of its groove) and into its place inside the oil pump body. Then check that the gears and keys are engaged on both sides of the pump by turning the shaft and trying to keep the gears from moving with your fingers.

As you install the oil pump's drive shaft through the crankcase bushing (first put some oil on the bushing) to position the oil pump against the crankcase, hold the pump body and gasket in place using two of the long oil pump bolts, which will allow you to move the pump around as needed.

Slip the oil pump's drive gear onto the end of the drive shaft, which is now inside the gearcase compartment of the engine, without the

woodruff key in the shaft. After turning the oil pump drive gear so the gear's slot aligns up with the keyway in the drive shaft, install the woodruff key into the slot and gear using a needlenose pliers that have some electric tape on its jaw tips. Do not put a mark on the key with the pliers.

Before you install the retaining ring onto the inner end of the drive shaft, rotate the gear and shaft so the keyway is 180 degrees away from where the opening of the retaining ring will be.

Once the pump is fully assembled onto the right crankcase, the six pump bolts must be torqued to spec in a specific procedure. With all six bolts loosely threaded in, slowly tighten them in a crisscross pattern. Alternate the bolts you tighten, bringing them down slowly as per the torquing procedure in the next paragraph. As you

15. *Slip the oil pump's drive gear onto the end of the drive shaft without the woodruff key in the shaft. Then install the woodruff key into the slot and gear using a needlenose pliers.*

16. *Install the retaining ring into its groove using a snap ring pliers and your finger. Once you've got it on, ensure that the snap ring is fully in its groove and fits snugly to the end of the shaft.*

tighten the bolts, turn the oil pump drive gear with your thumb to check for any binding. If the pump does start to bind, tap the pump body gently on the side to shift its position just a hair. All you're trying to do is reposition the body a few thousands of an inch, so the gears can turn smoothly again.

Here's the pump body bolt tightening procedure: Do a crisscross pattern with the four long bolts and torque them to 50 in-lbs. Then bring the top two bolts to 50 in-lbs. Next, torque the four bolts to 75 in-lbs. in the same pattern, then the top two. Go to the final torque of 110 in-lbs. in the same way. (H-D calls for 90-120 in-lbs.) After about an hour, retorque all six bolts to 110 in-lbs. (or 90-120) again following the same procedure since the gaskets will settle and the torque

may decrease. Whenever you're tightening a bolt, spin the oil pump drive gear with your finger to check for any hint of binding.

Once the pump body is flat against the crankcase, move the oil pump drive shaft in and out and use a flat feeler gauge to make sure you have 0.010"-0.025" of free movement. If you don't have the minimum, the pump will bind when the engine heats up. To fix the problem, you must remove the oil pump and take a little material from the shaft's brass bushing that's in the crankcase to get the needed clearance.

Oil enters the pump from the oil tank/pan through the feed fitting on the oil pump. Make sure you get this one right on both the tank/pan and pump, or your first startup is going to be short and expensive. On the stock pump, it's usu-

17. With the pump body flat against the crankcase, move the oil pump drive shaft in and out and use a flat feeler gauge to make sure you have 0.010"-0.025" of free movement.

18. Now thread the two top pump body bolts (blue Loctite on their threads) into the crankcase. We use a 3/16" Allen for ours. Leave the bolts loose for now.

ally the highest fitting on the pump's cover. However, you should check the manufacturer's manual covering the pump you're using to be sure. It's not the highest fitting in that corner of the engine, which is the one on the right crankcase; that's usually the vent fitting to the oil tank. On the S&S polished HVHP pump we're using for this chapter, it's either the top or bottom outside fitting/port on the pump cover or the fitting in the center of the pump cover. You get to choose which one is better for your application. However, you should check the detail instructions that came with your pump to be sure the same holds true for your pump. The return fitting on a stock H-D pump, which would go to the oil filter, is usually the one just below the feed fitting. Again, check the manual covering the year pump you're using to be sure.

On the S&S pump it's either the top or bottom inside fitting/port on the pump cover, your call.

Getting the fittings right on the pump and then hooking them up to the wrong fittings on the oil tank/pan is still going to cause problems. Be sure you know which fitting is for the feed, return, and vent lines on your tank/pan. Call the tank manufacturer if you're not absolutely certain. Or follow the test procedures in the last paragraph in the Oil Blow-By sidebar concerning how to check for an oil tank standpipe or hose connection problem.

If your engine is a crankcase breather and not a head breather, which has a port coming out of each head that connects to the air cleaner assembly, the lowest fitting on the crankcases should be vented to the atmosphere.

19. With a new gasket in place, install the oil pump cover using the four long bolts with blue Loctite on their threads. Leave the bolts loose for now. We used a 3/16" Allen.

20. Now torque all six pump bolts, as per the pump body bolt tightening procedure described in the Assembly Tips section of this chapter, as you turn the drive gear with your thumb to check for binding.

OIL BLOW-BY

Oil coming out of the lower end vent tube or out of the air cleaner (blow-by), depending on if it's top end or lower end vented, is a problem that has plagued the Evo from Day One. Though technically, this is not usually addressed in a book on how to build an engine, it is a known problem with Evo engines and some of the cures or preventative measures involve engine components, specifically the oil pump and oiling system.

The usual cause of oil blow-by is prolonged high-rpm engine speeds. The ascending and descending pistons and spinning flywheels whip the oil in the lower end into a mist. After a long time of elevated engine speeds, the engine's air/oil separation system is not able to remove this oily mist from the air that's being pushed out of the lower end vent system fast enough. It simply cannot keep up with demand. The result is an air/oil mist coming out of the lower end vent hose on a bottom breather engine (1984-92) or out of the breather ports in the heads, into the air cleaner assembly, and then onto the right side of the bike on a top breather (1993-99).

However, there are a number of mistakes that owners make that aggravate this problem. In fact, most owners that suffer with blow-by don't ride at sustained high speeds and, therefore, should not have the problem. Here are the common mistakes that owners make.

The first is the simplest to avoid and the easiest mistake to make: Overfilling the oil tank/pan. If there's too much oil in the tank/pan it allows oil into the tank's vent line and back into the engine's

21. Our S&S pump has options regarding feed and return oil line fitting locations. Seal the unused holes with a plug and some Teflon sealant. Also Teflon the threads of the fittings you install.

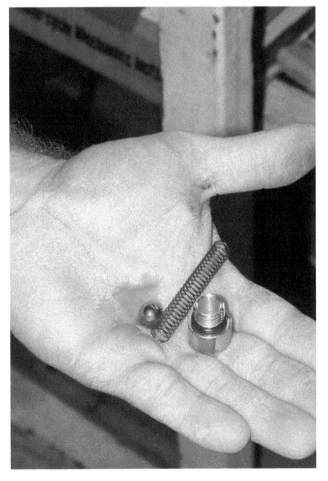

22. The components of the check valve are the check valve ball, a close-wound check valve spring, and the check valve spring cover, which should be installed with a new O-ring on it.

47

lower end. The excess oil prevents the engine and oil tank/pan from venting to each other correctly. The engine overfills with oil and then spits it out via any opening possible. There are a number of ways this can happen, with the first being keeping the oil level in the tank/pan too high. On many bikes, filling the oil tank/pan all the way up to the top oil fill line on the dipstick will create a blow-by problem. Resist the urge to keep adding oil to keep the oil level at maximum. Let the engine push out the oil it doesn't want and see if the oil level stabilizes at a point between the top line and the Add Oil line on the dipstick. If it does, make a new mark on the dipstick for your maximum oil fill line. Another way to overfill the tank/pan is to top it off after it has sat overnight or longer. Sometimes the check valve ball in the oil pump

will allow oil from the tank/pan to flow into the lower end of the engine. When you check the oil level it looks like it's low on oil, so you add some. Once you start the engine, the engine's oil pump returns the oil to the tank/pan, which is now overfilled. The same scenario happens if you don't run the engine before changing the oil and filter.

Since most Evo-powered bikes are rarely still with the original owner, a previous owner may have installed the wrong oil dipstick. The one you got with the bike may have the wrong oil level lines for your bike. The next time you change the oil and filter, refill the tank/pan with only three quarts of oil and then check the dipstick as per the recommended method for your year and model bike after you run the engine. The oil level should be near the Add Oil line of the dipstick. If

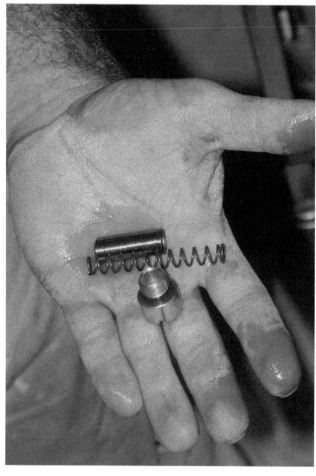

23. Once the check valve ball is in, followed by the check valve spring, install the check valve spring cover. Torque the spring cover to 80-110 in-lbs. using a large flat-bladed screwdriver.

24. The components of the oil pressure regulator are the relief valve, relief valve spring, and relief valve plug complete with new O-ring.

48

it's not, the dipstick is marked wrong for your bike. Make your own marks with the three-quart level being the Add Oil line. Then add another quart and, following the previous paragraph's instructions, find out where your bike wants its oil level.

If you have a bike that has a longer-than-stock front end on it, one that raises the front of the bike much higher than stock, the problem may be that now the dipstick is not reading the oil level in the tank correctly causing you to over-fill the oil tank/pan. Check for this in the same way you would check for an incorrect dipstick.

A slightly kinked, twisted, or collapsed bend in the oil return line (from the oil pump to the oil tank/pan) will restrict oil return to the tank/pan. The engine will not be able to send oil to the tank/pan as it should and will create the same overfilled lower end problem as described earlier.

Blow-by can also be caused by using the wrong oil filter. Twin Cam oil filters cannot be used on an Evolution engine. Though they will fit, they are too restrictive for an Evo oil system and will cause the same restriction as a kinked, twisted, or collapsed bend in the oil return line with the same result. A Twin Cam oil filter has a 5- or 10-micron filtering element while an Evolution uses a 30-micron element. Do not interchange them.

If your engine's oil pump is weak, installing an oil cooler may cause a blow-by problem. The oil pump may not be able to move oil through the oil filter and oil cooler fast enough to keep the engine from overfilling with oil.

25. First in is the relief valve, followed by the relief valve spring. The relief valve plug gets torqued to 80-110 in-lbs. using a large flat-bladed screwdriver.

26. Next in is the tappet oil screen and spring. The oil screen cap should also get a new O-ring and is also installed using a large flat-bladed screwdriver. Torque the cover to 80-110 in-lbs.

If the oil pump's return oil fitting is installed too deep into its elbow fitting on the pump, it will restrict return oil flow back to the tank/pan the same as a kinked, twisted, or collapsed oil line. To check for this, disconnect the oil return line from the oil pump and plug the hose. Now count how many threads are showing on the oil pump's oil return fitting. Then remove the fitting from its elbow fitting on the pump. Position the fitting alongside its elbow at the same thread depth it was when installed. Check inside the elbow to see if the inner end of the fitting was too deep in the elbow and covering part of the bend.

To check for an obstruction somewhere in the oil return system (the hoses, fittings, oil filter assembly, and, if installed, oil cooler), perform this test. Disconnect the oil return line from the oil pump and plug the hose. Then disconnect the return oil line from the oil tank/pan and plug it. Now run a new hose from the oil tank/pan directly to the oil return fitting on the oil pump. Ride the bike and see if the blow-by problem is fixed. If it is, identify the defective component by isolating each one and checking the system again.

An overfilled lower end can also be caused by defects in the left engine case; namely the same left crankcase machining and porosity defects listed in the Crankcase Concerns sidebar in Chapter 1: The Bottom End. Instead of allowing engine oil to overfill the primary cases, one or more of these same defects may be allowing primary case oil to seep into the engine's lower end causing the same problems as an overfilled oil tank/pan.

Another possible cause is a vent hose that's

27. Install the oil pump drive gear's key into the inner keyway on the pinion shaft. The key's flat side should protrude from the shaft about 1/32". Position the key in the inner most slot (arrow).

28. Slide the oil pump drive gear over the key (chamfer side facing in) and positioned so this gear engages the oil pump gear. Then rotate the engine and check for any sign of binding.

connected to the wrong port on the bottom of the oil tank or defective standpipes inside the oil tank. The oil tank has internal standpipes if there are two or three oil line connections on the bottom of the oil tank. If there is only one connection at the bottom of the tank it's for the oil feed line to the oil pump. The oil tank's internal vent and oil return standpipes must always be above the oil level in the tank even when the bike is leaned over in a turn. However, sometimes the internal vent standpipe is higher than the oil return standpipe. If the lines got switched and the tank is slightly overfilled, the vent line may be below the oil level creating the same problem as an overfill oil tank. An internal standpipe may also be defective in some way. It may have a hole, be bent over or broken loose from its attachment point in the tank.

To check for an oil tank standpipe or hose connection problem, first fill the oil tank to the proper level. Then disconnect the vent line from the engine's right crankcase and see if any oil comes out of it. Only a little oil should trickle out at the most from oil misting since no oil should be filling the vent line at any time. If a lot of oil comes out, something is wrong with its standpipe inside the tank or it's connected to the wrong fitting. Be sure to also lean the bike over as when in a turn as part of this test. Then disconnect the oil return line from the oil pump and let it drain into a jar. Only a little oil should trickle out, whatever was left in the line after the engine was shut off. Be sure to also lean the bike over for this test. If a lot of oil comes out, something is wrong with its standpipe inside the tank or it's connected to the wrong fitting. The oil feed line should always have oil in it, if connected to the right fitting on the tank.

29. *The oil pump is now properly assembled and installed onto the right crankcase, which means you're now ready to assemble the gearcase compartment as covered in Chapter 3.*

Chapter Three

The Gearcase Section

The driving force for the oil pump, ignition, and valvetrain

As mentioned in Chapter 1: The Bottom End, the driving force for the gearcase is the pinion shaft of the right flywheel. Every engine uses a large percentage of the power it produces to run itself. It is here, in the gearcase section, where some of the power created by the pistons on their power stroke is used to drive the oil pump, valvetrain, crankcase breather, and ignition system. Since this compartment contains the gears and shafts needed to do that the engineers call it the gearcase. (Engineers are very practical like that.) In older engines, the charging system, in the form of a generator, was also driven by

Breather gears come in plastic and metal versions. No matter which one you choose, the gear must be timed correctly.

the gearcase section. On 1970 and later Shovelheads, as well as all later Big Twin engines, the charging system is an alternator setup that's mounted behind the engine sprocket in the primary system and driven by the left flywheel's sprocket shaft.

The first gear that gets mounted on the pinion shaft, working our way from the inboard end out, is the oil pump drive gear, which engages the drive gear secured to the oil pump's drive shaft. This is the gear that, you guessed it, drives the oil pump. We installed this drive gear and the oil pump in Chapter 2: The Oil Pump. Next on the pinion shaft is the spacer, if you're using the pre-1990 pinion shaft and gears. On a 1990-99 oil pump drive gear, this spacer is part of that gear. The last gear on the pinion shaft is the pinion gear, which is the gear that drives the entire valvetrain via the camshaft gear. The inboard ends of both the pinion shaft and camshaft run in their own bearings in the right crankcase. The pinion shaft has a pinion bearing, which we installed in Chapter 1 and the camshaft has an inner camshaft bearing that we'll install in this chapter. The outboard ends of the pinion shaft and camshaft are supported by bushings in the cam (gearcase) cover. The cam cover's pinion bushing was reamed in Chapter 1, so it would be perfectly aligned with the pinion bearing race. This ensures the pinion shaft will not be preloaded when it's supported by its bearing and bushing. Preloading the pinion shaft because of a misalignment of its bearing and bushing causes excessive wear and a loss of horsepower due to excessive friction. These are two things we want to avoid in an engine, especially one we're hoping to make lots of power with. We did the same for the camshaft's cover bushing for the same reasons.

The camshaft is fitted with four odd-shaped lobes, the design of which many people devote their lives to understanding and improving. As complicated and consuming as any other mystery of the universe, the lift, duration, timing, lobe separation angle, and a number of other factors needed to make the best power with a particular combination of engine components and factors (intake airflow, compression ratio, cylinder bore, stroke, exhaust system, etc.) is not what we're going to cover here. As stated in the introduction, this book is about how to bake the cake, not what ingredients to put in it. Suffice to say, these magical little protrusions of metal control when, how high, and for how long each of the four valves in our Evo-style V-twin engine stay open and that's as far as we're going with them. These four cam lobes control the engine's four valves (two intakes and two exhausts, one of each per cylinder) via the valvetrain, which starts with the lifters and their lifter blocks. The lifter blocks are mounted on top of the right crankcase, right above the camshaft and just below the cylinders. Each block houses two lifters, one intake and one exhaust, which control the intake and exhaust valves for one cylinder. The lifters ride inside their blocks in fitted bores.

These lifters, also called tappets, are hydraulic units. Their main components are the roller, tappet body, and tappet. The roller is the wheel found at the bottom of the tappet body, which spins on a series of roller bearings. This roller is what rolls over the cam lobe, held there by the pressure exerted on it by the valve springs in the head. As the cam lobe profile rises and falls, so does the lifter in its lifter block. When the lobe profile rises it raises (lifts) the lifter and pushes the pushrod up to open its valve. When the lobe profile descends the lifter descends, which allows the valve springs to close the valve and push the pushrod back down.

SPECIAL TOOL LIST

Pinion gear puller
Pinion gear nut tool
Pinion gear locking tool
Cleaning tank
Compressed air supply
Inner cam bearing puller and installer
Emery paper (200-grit)
Steel straightedge
Teflon pipe sealant
Blue Loctite
Red Loctite
Section of 0.060"-thick wire (6"-long)
Section of 0.035"-thick wire (6"-long)
Two lifter block alignment tools

The tappet consists of a plunger (piston), cylinder, and check valve. The check valve is there so the tappet can pump itself up with engine oil and retain it for a time, which is what makes it different from the solid lifter assembly used by H-D on its older Big Twin designs. By pumping itself up, the lifter can take up the slack in the entire valvetrain, which consists of the cam lobe, lifter, pushrod, rocker arm, and valve stem end. How much slack there is in the valvetrain is a changing value. When the engine gets to operating temperature the aluminum cylinders and heads expand and grow taller, changing the distance from cam lobe to rocker arm, so the amount of slack in the valvetrain changes. The hydraulic lifters, when properly adjusted, pump themselves up to take up the slack and quiet down the valvetrain, as well as make it more efficient.

That is, except for the front exhaust pushrod. Though the lifter for that valve is doing its job, don't be surprised to find that part of the valvetrain still ticking away, no matter what you do. This is because of the extreme angle the front exhaust pushrod (the longest of the four) must operate at, reaching from the lifter by the centrally located cam to its rocker arm, which is the farthest one from the cam. This issue was addressed on the Twin Cams by using two cams in the gearcase instead of one. With two cams in the engine, the engineers could locate a cam directly under the two valves it controls, eliminating the extreme angle needed to operate the front exhaust valve found on all earlier H-D overhead valve Big Twin engines, and with it, that annoying tick!

A hydraulic lifter also has a specific bleed down rate, determined by its internal check valve, which is why the engine will tick when you first start it. The pressure of the valve springs has squeezed the oil out of some of the lifters' pistons, so there is excessive slack in the valvetrain. However, the lifters will pump themselves back up once they get a steady supply of pressurized oil.

This is where I plug an S&S product. No matter how mild or extreme you plan on building your engine, Reggie and I suggest you install an S&S HL2T Limiter kit into all four of your lifters. This kit, which consists of four small steel collars, corrects the two problems with the modern hydraulic lifter in H-D and similar aftermarket V-twin motors.

The other problem also involves the lifters bleeding down when you don't want them to, but this time it happens on the other end of the rpm range. Hotter cams require stronger valve springs, so the valves don't float when the engine's rpm are very high. But these stronger springs can also collapse hydraulic lifters when the engine is at high rpm. The S&S Limiter kit makes your hydraulic lifters act like solid lifters when you're trying to make the most power. At this point you may be thinking, if that's the case, why not just use solids in the engine? Solids can't pump up to take up the slack as an aluminum engine grows taller due to

The plastic breather gear (left) was used for all Evo Big Twin engines, while a steel one is used in earlier engines. When building your motor, we recommend using an aftermarket steel one.

heat expansion, which affects performance, as well as make the engine a lot noisier. Solid lifters are good for a dragstrip motor. The S&S HL2T kit eliminates the drawbacks of a hydraulic lifter. They'll still act like hydraulics when the engine is being operated normally, so there's no slack in the valvetrain. They'll also prevent the lifters from bleeding all the way down after the engine is shut off, so the valves will open normally when you fire off a cold engine. However, the lifters will be a little noisier than when stock and they do take a little longer to adjust once the HL2T is installed. You also must use adjustable pushrods with this kit. Installation consists of taking the lifter hydraulic unit and spring out of the lifter body, dropping in a HL2T collar, followed by the stock internal spring and the rest of the stock lifter assembly (see photo #12). As for the rest of the valvetrain, from the pushrods up, we'll cover them in Chapter 6: The Valvetrain.

Getting back to the pinion gear, it also drives the breather gear via the camshaft gear. The breather gear controls when return oil from the flywheel compartment is sent to the gearcase, so the scavenger side of the oil pump can send it through the oil filter and back to the oil tank/pan. The breather gear is also part of the crankcase venting system. As explained in Chapter 2: The Oil Pump, the rapidly descending pistons create positive pressure in the flywheel compartment, which forces the return oil from the flywheel compartment through the breather gear that's timed to open when the pistons descend and into the gearcase compartment. The scavenger side of the oil pump can then remove the unwanted oil from the engine.

CHANGES

On pre-1993 Evos, the engine vents excessive positive pressure from the flywheel

and gearcase compartments to the atmosphere via a vent in the right crankcase, as shown in Chapter 1: The Bottom End. H-D changed the design of its engine for the 1993 models. On these and all later Evos, the pressurized oily mist from the lower end is sent to the rocker boxes where the oil is separated from the air. The now oil-free pressurized air is then vented into the air cleaner via a port in the right side of each head and drawn back into the engine to be burned in the combustion chambers. We'll cover the changes in the top end in more detail in Chapter 6: The Valvetrain. For now, let's look at how this resulted in some changes in the components of the gearcase section, as well as some other modifications H-D made over the years. We'll start with the pinion gear and shaft, though shaft changes are also noted in Chapter 1: The Bottom End. As for the different versions of oil pump drive gears, they are covered in Chapter 2: The Oil Pump.

There are three different pinion shafts used in the Evo. The first one, used from 1984 to 1989 (#24006-83), has a tapered end for the pinion gear and two keyways with woodruff keys (#23985-54/#26348-15), one for the pinion gear and one for

The cam cover was changed for 1993 due to the new head breather bolt crankcase venting configuration. The early cam cover (left) has a baffle in the upper left corner and a breather tube in its lower right corner.

the oil pump drive gear (#26349-73). The oil hole for the shaft and flywheel is 90 degrees off from the woodruff key slot. This pinion shaft version also has its oil feed hole in the center of the tapered end that goes into the cam cover. It uses a left-hand thread pinion gear nut (#24023-54) and a flywheel nut (#24016-80) with a woodruff key (#11218). This shaft's pinion gear uses a separate spacer (#24703-54) between it and the oil pump drive gear. This pinion shaft is the strongest of the three and the one to use in a high performance engine. The next shaft style was used on 1990-92 Evos and is part of the right flywheel. This shaft is the same length as the earlier one, but it does not have a tapered end (see photo). It also has only one keyway, which takes a special elongated woodruff key that drives both the pinion gear and oil pump drive gear and uses a left-hand

1. If you have not already done it, change out the stock INA inner cam bearing for a Torrington one. Reggie prefers to do this using an inner cam bearing puller and installer.

pinion gear nut. The oil pump drive gear for this style shaft has an integral spacer, not a separate one. The late-style 1993-99 pinion shaft is longer than both earlier shafts and is also part of the right flywheel. However, it, like the 1990-92 shaft, is not tapered, has a single keyway, and uses the post-1990 oil pump drive gear with integral spacer. It has a different pinion gear, one that doesn't have a counterbore on its face. It uses a right-hand (standard) threaded nut as opposed to the earlier designs with their left-hand thread.

The 1977 to 1989 pinion gear comes in seven different fitment sizes and has a single circular line cut into its face for identification. (Aftermarket vendors, like S&S, usually offer only four different sizes.) The 1990 and all later pinion gears (both versions) come in twice as many fitment sizes and have two circular lines cut into its face for identification. The increase in fitment sizes was done to get better pinion gear-to-camshaft gear fitment and reduce gear noise. The different sizes are identified by different colors.

A steel breather gear is used in all overhead valve H-D engines up to early-1977. From late-1977 to 1999, Harley used different black plastic versions in its Big Twins. Harley's seven-slot black plastic version, and its earlier steel breather gear are for use only in bikes with a dry clutch setup, such as the Shovelhead-powered machines and some Evos with a four-speed transmission where the primary drive's oiling system is part of the engine oiling system. The stock black plastic #253130-77B breather gear was used in the early-1984 dry clutch bikes and in 1984-86 wet clutch bikes. The six-slotted black plastic #25310-82A breather gear's use started in 1987 and continued until 1991. In 1991, Harley came out with another plastic version (#25311-90), which can be retrofitted back to 1984 on all wet clutch bikes. However, the factory went back to using the #25310-82A breather gear after a short time and continued its use from late-1992 until 1999. If you're going to use a black plastic breather gear, install the #25311-90 breather gear in all wet clutch-equipped 1984 to early-1992 bikes and the #25310-82A breather gear in a late-1992 to 1999 engine.

That said, Reggie Jr. recommends that you do not use the black plastic breather gear that came with any stock Evo engine. Sometimes they are badly out of round, which hampers proper oil scavenging of the flywheel compartment. The plastic gears also have a bad habit of catching carbon chips, which get embedded in the plastic and then scratch and gall the breather gear well in the right crankcase. If the damage to the crankcase well is too severe, you must replace the entire right crankcase half. And that would suck almost as bad as a seared oil pump key. Thankfully, JIMS sells a 0.030" oversize steel breather gear, so you can have a slightly scoured breather gear well in the crankcase machined clean. JIMS also sells the tool needed to do this repair. The better way is to use a steel breather gear, like the ones offered by JIMS or S&S Cycle. Of course, these problems don't happen to all plastic breather gears, but it is a known issue. I've also heard good things about S&S Cycle's reed breather gear (#31-2096), though I have not used one myself. This setup may also be used in a badly scoured breather well. It has also been known to help reduce oil blow-by out of a head-breathing 1993 and later engine.

As for the cam cover, there are only two versions and it's easy to tell them apart (see photo). The 1984-92 version has a baffle plate in its top right corner (when on the engine), which helps separate oil from the pressurized air that's trying to make its way out of the engine's crankcases. An internal tube (or air duct tube) sends this now less-oily air down to a tube that protrudes from the cam cover and goes into a hole in the lower left corner of the gearcase section of the right case. This hole is connected to the vent fitting that's inboard and below the oil pump on the outside of the right crankcase. A hose connects this fitting to the air cleaner housing, so the mist from the engine can be sucked into the engine and burned during the combustion event. The 1993-99 version doesn't have the baffle plate or air duct tube.

PREP WORK

Start by checking that all passageways in the cam cover and both lifter blocks are clean and clear of debris, be it metal filings, small bits of packing material, or carbon and/or dirt in a used part. Use a stiff bristle bottlebrush, a cleaning tank, and some compressed air to clean out all passageways. The ones in the crankcases should have already been checked and

cleaned as described in Chapter 1: The Bottom End.

Check all threaded holes. Make sure they are free of debris and dirt. Make sure all threads are in good shape and will not strip out when you reinstall whatever goes into them at the correct torque. Now is the time to weld up, machine flat, drill, and tap new threads into a stripped hole if not already done.

Put all the new bushings and bearings you plan on installing in a freezer until the exact moment you plan on installing them. Making them very cold reduces their ID slightly and makes it easier to install them, as does a slight coat of light oil. This also causes less wear to the walls of the hole in your crankcases, cam cover, or whatever main engine part you're installing the new bushing/bearing into since the new part doesn't rub against the walls as much.

2. With the pre-1990 pinion shaft and gear, install the pinion gear spacer against the oil pump drive gear installed in Chapter 2. On 1990-99 Evos, this spacer is part of the oil pump drive gear.

After spraying a shop cloth with brake clean, wipe off the gasket surfaces of the cam cover, right crankcase, and both lifter blocks to remove any dirt or oily residue. Then check that all gasket surfaces are free of gouges, imprints, marks with depth (if you can feel it with your fingernail, it's too deep), or any other imperfections that may allow oil to get past the gaskets. Check out the Gasket Help sidebar if you do find some imperfections. Also check all four lifters and the bores of both lifter blocks for gouges, scouring marks with depth, or any other imperfections that may cause a problem. Do the same for the bushings in the cam cover.

Check the fit of all the woodruff keys in their slots, both on the shafts and gears. Make sure the keys fit into their slot with finger pressure or just a little looser. If the key fits too tightly, sand both sides with 200-grit emery paper until it slides smoothly into its keyway. Then make sure the flat side of the key protrudes up from the shaft at least 1/32" when it's fully seated in its slot.

Check that the oil passages on the cam cover and lifter blocks lines up with the ones on the crankcase. Do this by laying the new gasket against the parts in question and then the crankcase. If the holes in the part and crankcase line up with the holes in the gasket, you're all set. If not, find out why and correct the problem. Hopefully, you just have the wrong gasket and not the wrong part.

Check the condition of all the parts you plan on installing in this phase of the build. If you plan on reusing old parts, you must check all dimensions as per the engine manufacturer's spec. Also check all dimensions if you're using new components. Then check that the clearances are correct between the two parts when they're assembled as per the manufacturer's specs. This is the blueprinting part of the process. Parts are mass produced and made to be a certain size, within a tolerance range, maybe +/- 0.001, more or less. Say the used lifter blocks you plan on using are within H-D wear specs but on the looser end of the acceptable size range for that part. And the new lifters you plan on using are also within usable specs but on the smaller diameter end of the acceptable spec range. When you check the fit of the new lifter in its bore in the used lifter block, you may get a very loose fit of 0.0025", which is outside the acceptable range of 0.0008"- 0.002" and almost where replacement is recommended (over 0.003"). Why install a part that's almost too loose before the engine has even been started? Replace the lifter block or use a different new lifter in that bore, one that is on the larger end of that part's acceptable size range. Thankfully, this should not be as much as a problem now as it was a decade or more ago thanks to better manufacturing processes that produce parts with tighter tolerances.

Look for signs of scuffing or pitting on all components. Any grooves or scoring on the body of a lifter or in the bore of a lifter block is cause for concern. If you can feel the mark with your fingernail, it's too deep to reuse. Replace the defective part. Do

3. After inserting the woodruff key into its slot in the pinion shaft, slip the pinion gear onto its shaft. Ensure the gear fits somewhat snug onto its shaft and key, and goes against the pinion gear spacer.

the same for all cam cover bushings (Chapter 1: The Bottom End tells you how to replace them) and the cam itself, as well as the breather gear, and all thrust washers and shims. Measure the cam to make sure it's within useable specs. Take a measurement on the inboard end of the cam (bearing journal) where it runs in the bearing. Then take a measurement near the inboard cam lobe, where the cam has not been running inside a bearing but it's still the bearing journal. If the difference is more than 0.003", replace the cam. Also replace the cam if any of the lobes are pitted, worn, have grooves, etc., where the roller contacts the lobe. If the hardened surface of the cam lobes or bearing journal is worn down at all, replace the cam. Check the teeth on the breather, camshaft, and pinion gears for wear. Replace the part if you find any that have worn a crease in the teeth or the hardened outer skin has been worn through.

After cleaning the lifters' rollers with contact cleaner, check each roller's fit and end clearance. If they are past the manufacturer's specs, replace it. H-D calls for replacement if this exceeds 0.0015" and 0.015", respectively. Personally, unless the lifter has only a couple thousand miles on it, I'd never reuse an old lifter assembly, since a bad one can cause severe damage. (Check out the Lifter Tips sidebar.) Check the fit of the lifter in its bore. H-D calls for a loose fit of 0.0008"- 0.002". According to H-D, if it exceeds 0.003" replace it. Also check the fit of the lifter block in the right crankcase. H-D also calls for a loose fit here: 0.000"- 0.004". H-D's spec for the inboard end of the cam in its bearing is 0.0005"- 0.0025". And don't even think about reusing old inner cam bearings! Replace them with quality bearings; it's cheap insurance against a premature failure.

4. The pinion gear nut gets threaded onto the pinion shaft next. But don't torque it down just yet, since you may have to change the pinion gear. Leave the nut only finger tight at this time.

5. A steel breather gear goes into the well in the right crankcase next. Don't worry about the timing mark; we'll get to that later.

ASSEMBLY TIPS

When replacing the inner cam bearing located in the right crankcase, do not use a stock INA bearing in either a stock or high performance engine. Install a Torrington one. Here's why: H-D changed to the caged INA bearing in mid-1992 for alignment reasons. The INA has 19 needle rollers that are separated from each other by the cage that holds them. The bearing's construction allows it to be more forgiving of a misalignment between the bearing and the cam bushing in the cam cover. That was something, I guess, H-D wanted in its mass-produced engines back then. The Torrington bearing has 29 needle rollers and is a much stronger bearing, which is what you need and want, especially when running higher pressure valve springs. As for the alignment issue, if you're running the same cam cover, your alignment

should be fine. However, if you're also rebuilding the lower end, this is the time to have the cam cover bushing reamed in alignment with the inner cam bearing to be sure. Ditto for the cam cover's pinion shaft bushing in relation to the pinion bearing. (This is all covered in Chapter 1: The Bottom End.) When fully installed (writing on the bearing facing out), the new inner cam bearing should not protrude from its hole. It should be just below the wall of the right crankcase and just touching the ridge in the back of its hole.

When selecting the proper breather gear shim, place a steel straightedge across the gasket surface of the gearcase compartment and use a flat feeler gauge to measure the endplay between the random test shim you placed on the end of the breather gear and the straightedge. You want about 0.011"- 0.021" at

6. *Pick any thickness breather shim and place it on the breather gear, since you're going to check its end-play next. Then put a new cam cover gasket on the right crankcase.*

7. *Use a steel straightedge and flat feeler gauge to measure the endplay between the test breather gear shim and straightedge. You want about 0.011"-0.021" at this time, since the gasket is not yet crushed.*

60

this time, since the gasket is not yet crushed. When the cam cover is torqued to spec you'll lose about 0.006" of endplay. Final endplay range is usually 0.005"- 0.015" on an aftermarket engine, while Harley calls for 0.001"- 0.016". The final endplay you want is about 0.006" - 0.008", so you're looking to have about 0.012" - 0.014" now.

When checking for proper gear lash between the pinion gear and camshaft, most mechanics use special pins and do a shitload of measuring. While that's the H-D recommended method (you can see how to do this in Chapter 7: Special Procedures), and it will get you where you want to go, a much better and easier way is to just use your fingers. Here's how Reggie Jr. does it: With the cam cover installed and the camshaft engaged with the pinion gear, put your fingers through the lifter block holes in the right

crankcase and see how hard it is to move camshaft in and out. You have the proper fit if you feel a slight drag as the camshaft's teeth slide back and forth past the pinion gear's teeth, without any real resistance. If you have to force the camshaft to move, the fit is too tight and you need to install the next size smaller pinion gear. A looser, sloppy fit requires a larger pinion gear. Reggie recommends starting with a red dot pinion gear, which is a middle size, and working from there, if needed. Most aftermarket cams come with a drive gear matching a middle (red) pinion gear. You should check the gear lash of the camshaft to the pinion gear at these four positions of flywheel rotation, for two full rotations of the flywheel assembly, for a total of eight positions: Top Dead Center (TDC), Bottom Dead Center (BDC), and the two positions halfway between them, which is when the

8. With just the camshaft thrust washer on the inboard end of the cam, slip the cam into the inner cam bearing. Don't bother with lube or the timing marks on the pinion and breather gears; we're only checking fitment.

9. After removing the test breather gear shim, the cam cover is installed and its bolts just snugged down. Don't crush the gasket at this point, since we're still taking measurements.

crankpin is at a 90-degree angle to the sprocket and pinion shafts. Don't check the gear lash at only some flywheel positions; do the full range.

To get the correct camshaft endplay, don't try to take the short cut of just measuring the length of the old and new camshafts and figuring out the shim needed for the new camshaft based on the difference in length between the two. The stock 1990 and later Evos have a much looser endplay spec than all after-market cam manufacturers require. Even the stock endplay spec for the 1984-89 Evos is probably different than spec required by your new camshaft.

So, to get the correct camshaft endplay, move the cam as far away from the right case (outboard) as possible. Slip a flat feeler gauge into the gap between the inboard end of the cam and its thrust washer to see how much total endplay you have. The correct

size shim to put between the thrust washer and cam is the size of this gap, minus the required endplay, minus what you're going to lose to gasket crush once the cam cover is torqued to spec. Let's say the total endplay is 0.042". Since we want a total final endplay of about 0.012" and we're going to lose about 0.006" when the gasket is crushed on final assembly, 0.024" worth of shims (or as close as you can get to that) would go between the thrust washer and inboard end of the camshaft. The formula for this is 0.042" (Measured Inboard Endplay) - 0.012" (Final Total Endplay) - 0.006" (Gasket Crush) = 0.024" (Inboard Shims Needed). Once you reinstall the cam cover and torque the bolts to spec, recheck the endplay before proceeding with the build.

Here's how to get the correct camshaft endplay and align the cam lobes with the lifter rollers. Move

10. The first check is for proper gear lash between the pinion gear and camshaft gear. Most mechanics use special pins, but the easier way is to just use your fingers as outlined in Assembly Tips.

11. The next measurement is camshaft endplay. Slip a flat feeler gauge into the gap between the inboard end of the cam and its thrust washer. Then follow the procedure outlined in Assembly Tips.

the cam as far away from the right case (outboard) as possible. Slip a flat feeler gauge into the gap between the inboard end of the cam and its thrust washer to see how much total endplay you have. In our engine, the total endplay was 0.042". Then move the cam so its lobes align with the rollers of the two lifters. Carefully measure what the gap between the inboard end of the cam and its thrust washer is now, while still keeping the lobes aligned with their lifter rollers. Ours was 0.019". Then remove the cam cover, so you can shim both sides of the cam to get the proper overall endplay, as well as keep the cam's lobes aligned to the lifter rollers. To do this, you must put a normal cam shim between the thrust washer and cam that's the size of this gap, minus half of the required endplay, minus half of what you're going to lose to gasket crush once the cam cover is torqued to spec.

The gap between the inboard end of the cam and its thrust washer when the cam lobes were aligned to their lifter rollers on our engine was 0.019". Since we want a total final endplay of 0.012" and we're going to lose 0.006" when the gasket is crushed on final assembly, a 0.010" shim would go between the thrust washer and inboard end of the camshaft. The formula for this is 0.019" (Measured Inboard Endplay) - 0.006" (Half Of 0.012" Wanted Total Endplay) - 0.003" (Half Of 0.006" Gasket Loss) = 0.010" (Inboard Shim Needed). Since the total cam endplay measurement we got in step 11 was 0.042", we're left with a cam endplay of 0.023" on the outboard end of the camshaft to deal with. The formula to figure out what size shim to use here is: 0.023" (Remaining Endplay) - 0.006" (Half Of 0.012" Wanted Total Endplay) - 0.003" (Half Of 0.006" Gasket Loss) =

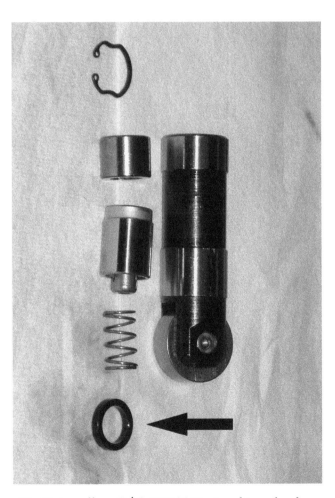

12. To install an S&S HL2T Limiter kit, take the internal components out of the lifter body, drop in the S&S Limiter collar (arrow), and reinstall the stock lifter assembly components.

13. You can now lube and install the lifters into their blocks. Reggie always puts the oil hole on the lifter body facing the engine (inboard).

0.014" (Outboard Shim Needed). We need to put a 0.014"-thick shim on the outboard end of the camshaft to get the 0.012" total endplay we want once the cam cover is torqued down, while still keeping the lifter rollers aligned with their cam lobes. This second shim goes between the outboard end of the camshaft and the cam cover. Since a standard cam shim will not fit over the outer end of the camshaft, Reggie uses a 0.030"-thick Timken bearing shim (#TRA 1625). Though we only need a 0.014"-thick shim, Reggie feels a shim thinner than 0.030" would be too weak. His fix is to machine some material off the outer face of the camshaft's cam cover bushing. In this case, we need to machine off 0.016" to get the proper clearance. You may not have to machine anything off the cam cover bushing, or put an outer shim in at all, so run the clearance and alignment

checks before you machine the cam cover bushing. Once you've installed the shims, reinstalled the cam cover and recheck the endplay and lifter-to-lobe alignment as you did before, before proceeding with the build.

With the camshaft properly shimmed and cam cover installed with the cover bolts just snugged since we're still taking measurements, it's time to check the gap between the inner most cam lobe and the curved ridge in the right crankcase. (If you rebuilt the lower end as per Chapter 1, you've already checked this clearance but you may want to double check it now since the cam is now properly shimmed.) This upward curved ridge is just above the pinion bearing and just below the inner camshaft bearing. The check is done through one of the lifter block holes in the right crankcase using a 0.035"-thick wire. Thankfully,

14. With new gaskets on the crankcase, install the blocks using two lifter block alignment tools. Just snug the bolts down for now. We're still checking fitments, so we don't want to crush the gasket yet.

15. Note how this cam's lobes and lifter rollers are aligned. To do the same, follow the procedure outlined in Assembly Tips. Then remove the lifters and blocks, cam cover, breather shim, and camshaft with shims.

unless you're going to use a high-lift radical cam, there's usually enough clearance here, but you should check it anyway to be sure. Rotate the engine so the innermost cam lobe has its peak right above this curved ridge in the right crankcase. Now pass the 0.035"-thick wire, which is the minimum clearance you want here when the cam cover gasket is not crushed, between all sides of the peak of the cam lobe and the ridge. More than 0.035" clearance is fine. If you have less, you'll need to machine the section of the right crankcase that's too close to the cam lobe to get the clearance you need. If you do have to machine some material off the right crankcase, remove the camshaft and its shims, and the breather gear. Place some duct tape over the inner cam bearing to keep metals shavings out. Drape a thick oily rag over the pinion bearing and shaft, as well as over

the breather gear well in the right case. Use a rag large enough to completely cover everything under the area or near the area you're going to clearance. Once done, make sure there's no metal debris or shavings left in the gearcase compartment.

To check the cam lobe-to-lifter roller clearances (see photo 20), install one of the lifter and lifter block assemblies. Then rotate the engine so one of the cam lobes has its peak right under the lifter roller it controls. Then pull the lifter up to the top of its slot in the lifter block, which is the highest it can go, with your fingers. Now pass a 0.060"-thick wire, which is the minimum clearance you want here, between the roller and the peak of the cam lobe. More than 0.060" clearance is fine. If you have less, you'll need to machine the slot in the lifter block to get the clearance you need. Check all four lifters in their blocks

16. After installing the correct pinion gear, if needed, put some red Loctite on the pinion nut, install a pinion gear locking tool, and torque the pinion nut to 35-45 ft-lbs. using a pinion nut tool.

17. With assembly lube on the inner cam bearing, breather gear, and breather well, slip the proper shims onto the camshaft and the breather gear. Reinstall the camshaft, but don't bother with the timing marks yet.

65

in the same way. If you do have to machine some material off a lifter block, make sure you wash it thoroughly afterwards and clean all oil passageways of dirt and machining debris.

To check the cam lobe-to-lifter block clearances (see photo 21), install one of the lifter and lifter block assemblies. Then rotate the engine so one of the cam lobes has its peak right under the lifter block of the roller it controls. Then, using the same 0.060"-thick wire, check for at least that much clearance between the highest point of the cam lobe and the bottom of the lifter block. More than 0.060" clearance is fine. If you have less, you'll need to machine the section of the lifter block that's too close to the cam lobe to get the clearance you need. Check both cam lobes for each lifter block in the same way. If you do have to machine some material off a lifter block, make sure

you wash it thoroughly afterwards and clean all oil passageways of dirt and machining debris.

GASKET HELP

What do you do if there are gasket surfaces that have gouges, imprints, marks with depth (if you can feel it with your fingernail, it's too deep), or any other imperfections that may allow oil to get past the gaskets? If the damage is too deep to be sealed with the gasket (which depends on the gasket you use), putting a skin coat of clear RTV may solve the problem.

By skin coat, I mean a very thin coat of RTV only on the damaged area. Don't be the guy who uses so much RTV some of it squeezes out from between the gasket and parts being sealed. Not only is the RTV squeezing out where you can see and remove the excess. It's doing the same thing on the inside of

18. *Reinstall the cam cover again but just snug the bolts, since we're still taking measurements. Use a flat feeler gauge to check the end gap of the cam, which should be about 0.018" with an uncrushed gasket.*

19. *With gaskets on the case, reinstall one of the lifter block assemblies using two lifter block alignment tools. Just snug the bolts down again (don't crush the gasket), since we're still taking measurements.*

the engine where you can't remove the excess. That internal extra RTV may break loose and clog a vital small oil passage, restricting or stopping oil flow causing who know what kind of damage. It's like giving your engine a partial stroke.

Of course, a deep imperfection may be beyond this simple repair trick and require welding and machining to make the gasket surface smooth again.

LIFTER TIPS

Though the modern hydraulic lifter used in Evo-style engines is pretty much an install-it-and-forget-it item for the most part, they, like all moving parts, do wear out. There are two ways they can fail, one starts with a light tapping to warn you, and when it does fail it doesn't do a lot of damage. Though it can leave you stranded on the side of the road. The other is also noisy, but by the time you hear it, the damage to

other parts (remember what I told you in Chapter 2: The Oil Pump?) may already be done.

Let's take the easy one first, which involves the tappet section, specifically the piston, which is sometimes called a plunger. When this fails, the lifter can't take up the slack in the valvetrain as it should, so you hear a light tapping or ticking on the right side of the engine. After a while, as the lifter fails more, the engine gets harder to start, the noise gets louder, and you start to lose power. If it fails completely, as in it no longer opens the valve it controls, you'll find yourself stranded on the side of the road. Tappet failure is due to piston wear in its bore in the tappet and the associated oil pressure loss. If the tappet can't maintain a pumped up state, it can't open its valve as it should. However, this can also occur in a good lifter if dirt or debris gets into the lifter and clogs it.

20. Are the rollers aligned with their lobes? Then rotate the engine and check the clearance between the highest point of each cam lobe and its lifter using a 0.060"-thick wire as per the Assembly Tips procedure.

21. Again, rotate the engine and check the clearance between the highest point of each cam lobe and the bottom of its lifter block using the 0.060"-thick wire as per the Assembly Tips procedure.

Low oil pressure, whether due to the oil pump or a clogged lifter oil screen, will also cause poor lifter operation.

As for the other failure possibility, that happens on the other end of the lifter. The roller, which follows the cam lobe, is supported by many tiny roller bearings. And, like all bearings, they wear out and fail if not replaced. The problem is that when the roller fails a loose bearing can fall out of the roller and get jammed between the teeth of the oil pump gear and its drive gear, or the breather gear and camshaft gear, etc. Jam the oil pump and, as explained in Chapter 2, no more oil flows in or out of the engine; either one is bad. (Truth is, the bearing usually finds its way into the oil pump gears.) Even if the bearing doesn't jam a set of gears, you don't want slivers and bits of metal circulating through your engine, galling every-

thing they encounter. If the roller, or a piece of it, gets lodged between the breather gear and its well, it could trash the entire right crankcase.

Want to avoid both of these unpleasant scenarios? Change your oil and filter regularly and clean the lifter oil screen at least at every second oil change. And when it's time, change the lifters out before they go belly up. The common rule of thumb for a performance engine is to change the entire lifter group, all four of them, every 20,000-25,000 miles.

When removing the lifters from their blocks for any reason other than replacement, number them and note their orientation. You should always put a used lifter back into the same lifter bore and orientate it the same as before whenever you reassembled a previously-run engine. Reggie always puts the oil hole on the lifter body facing the engine (inboard). This

22. After removing the lifters, lifter blocks, and cam cover, install a new seal into the cam cover. You don't want to do this earlier, since you may damage the seal while doing all the clearance checks.

23. After lubing both ends of the camshaft, reinstall the cam with all its shims and thrust washer. Make sure all the timing marks are properly aligned to the breather and pinion gears as shown.

way if he takes an engine apart (maybe to change the cam), the lifter will always go in the same way so its roller will be turning in the same direction as before.

CAMSHAFT BASICS

Though we're not going to get into what camshaft profiles should be used with a certain combination of performance engine components, a discussion of camshaft basics is needed, since the cam you choose affects what must be done to your engine's heads.

The shape of a camshaft's lobe determines a number of valvetrain events: when the valve will open, how far it will open, how long it will stay open, when it will close, and how quickly it will open and close. When most beginning builders talk about cams, they usually discuss lift, which is how far the cam lobe will open the valve it controls. This is expressed in decimal fractions of an inch, such as .600". We'll discuss where this measurement is taken, as well as a number of other factors, in Chapter 6: The Heads. Though lift does have a lot to do with how the engine will perform, how long it will stay open, which is called duration, probably plays a greater role in engine performance. A cam's duration is based on when the lobe opens the valve and when it allows it to close. These are measured by degrees of flywheel rotation, as explained in Chapter 1: The Bottom End. The sections of the lobe that actually open the valve and then slow it down before it closes back onto its seat are called the ramps. The last term you should know at this point is valve overlap, which is the period of time when both valves in a head are open at the same time.

24. After lubing the end of the pinion shaft and all cover bushings, with the new gasket on the case and a little oil on the seal, reinstall the cover and torque the bolts to 11-13 ft-lbs. H-D calls for 90-120 in-lbs.

25. Check the camshaft's endplay once more using a flat feeler gauge. It should be about 0.012" with a crushed gasket. Also use a pick tool to make sure the breather gear still has some endplay.

26. With the lifters lubed, reinstall the lifter block assemblies with blue Loctite on the bolts, using 2 lifter block alignment tools. Most aftermarket engines torque the bolts to 11-13 ft-lbs.; H-D wants 12-15 ft-lbs.

Chapter Four

The Pistons & Cylinders

The components that are your motor's muscle

Some people like to refer to the pistons and cylinders as an engine's lungs. And while I can see why they think that, for me, the piston, as it moves in its cylinder, is an engine's muscle. Sure, it acts like a lung, drawing in fresh air and then blowing it back out once it's done with it, but that's just what it does before and after its main purpose. And a piston's main purpose is to produce power! In fact, creating power is the only reason for the engine's existence. The piston, moving down on its power stroke, is what it's all

A modern piston has a compression ring located in each of the two grooves near the top of the piston. The three-piece oil control ring lives just below the second compression ring, in the wider groove.

The underside of a piston, which is exposed to the oil that's splashed around in the lower end, is built up around the wrist pin for structural integrity. The gap between the two supports is for the top of the connecting rod.

about when it comes to a reciprocating internal combustion engine. Everything else is there to either enable that to happen or send that power on its way to the rear wheel. I think that's why some motorheads tattoo a set of crossed pistons on their bicep instead of valves or some other engine component. Now that we've established the piston as the head honcho of the internal combustion engine universe, let's discuss its job and main sections, as well as its different shapes and types.

To make power, an internal combustion engine burns (not explodes) a mixture of fuel and air inside its cylinders. In fact, it should be a fast burn, since a slow burn results in lower power output and a hotter running engine. The cylinder makes up the sides of the containment area where the fuel/air mixture is brought for burning. The head's combustion chamber forms the top of this area, while the piston forms the bottom. However, to do its job, the piston is a moving wall that helps draw in the mixture, get rid of the burnt gases, and, most importantly, changes the heat, and therefore, pressure formed by the burning mixture into mechanical energy. The piston, in preparation for the combustion event, also compresses the fuel/air mixture to increase the amount of power it will produce when ignited. How much the mixture is compressed when the piston is at the top of its stroke is called the engine's static compression ratio. This is simply the ratio of the volume of the combustion chamber plus the volume (displacement) of the cylinder when the piston is at the bottom of its stroke, called Bottom Dead Center (BDC), compared to the volume of the combustion chamber plus the volume of the cylinder when the piston is at the top of its stroke, called Top Dead Center (TDC). At TDC, all or almost all of the volume of the cylinder has been compressed into the area of the combustion chamber, since the top of the piston stops right at or very close to the top of the cylinder. For example, let's use an engine where the

flattop piston stops right at the top edge of the cylinder. If the cylinder's displacement is 670cc and the size of the combustion chamber is 78cc, the engine's static compression ratio is 670 plus 78 divided by 78, which equals 748/78 or 9.6:1.

A piston has different sections to it that do different tasks. Starting at the top, an Evo-style piston's head (or crown) is usually flat and stops right at or very near the top edge of the cylinder. Sometimes it may have a dome that protrudes into the combustion chamber to increase the engine's compression ratio. However, a builder can also use a flattop piston and mill the heads and/or cylinders to increase the compression ratio. (We'll get into milling, also called decking, in Chapter 7: Special Procedures.) A dished crown piston is usually used on a very large displacement engine. Since they must compress lots more cubic inches into the combustion chamber, the top of this piston is relieved to drop the static compression ratio down to a useable level. The top of a piston usually has two half-circle grooves cut into it to give the intake and exhaust valves needed clearance.

SPECIAL TOOL LIST

Parts cleaning tank
Compressed air supply
Blue Loctite
Piston ring compressor
Wrist pin clip installer
Piston ring grinding tool
Cylinder bore gauge or micrometer
Large 5" micrometer or dial indicator
Piston ring compressor
Cylinder stud installation/removal tool
About 2' of 3/8" ID rubber hose

The cylinder-shaped side of the piston has three grooves cut into it that run parallel to the top for the entire circumference of the piston. These grooves are where the piston rings go. The spaces between the grooves are the rings lands. The modern motorcycle piston has two compression rings near the top and a single three-piece oil control ring just below the second compression ring, but above the wrist pin holes. The oil ring's groove has

Here are three pistons with different head (crown) shapes. On the left is a domed piston, in the middle is the flattop piston commonly used, and on the right is a dished piston for very large displacement engines.

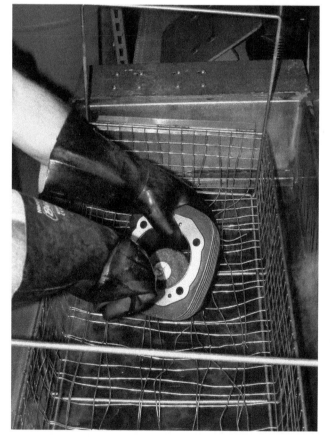

Assembly sequence #1

1. Once the cylinders have been machined, thoroughly wash them with hot water and soap, including all oil passageways. Then rinse with fresh water and blow them clean and dry with compressed air.

holes in it to help surplus oil, scraped from the cylinder bore, return to the lower end. The compression rings are needed because, though a piston is a tight fit to its cylinder, it's not tight enough to keep the pressure generated during combustion in the chamber above. The oil rings are there to keep the oil from the flywheel compartment below out of the combustion chamber. To do this, all the rings must fit against the cylinder walls very tightly and be at the exact same arc as the curve of the cylinder walls. They must also be able to press out against the cylinder walls with equal force at all points. A piston's rings also help transfer heat from the piston to the cylinder, so it can be dissipated to the surrounding air via the cylinder's cooling fins.

The compression rings must also maintain a gas-tight fit against the ring lands above and below them. The cross section of a compression ring is either rectangular or wedged-shaped with a tapered face, depending on the manufacturer's design. The oil rings are usually comprised of two thin strips of steel with a ridged expander that helps the oil rings maintain shape and position. The oil rings must allow a thin film of oil to pass by them and stay on the cylinder walls to lubricate and help seal the piston and cylinder. However, if too much oil is left on the walls, the engine will smoke and leave a thick carbon residue on the top of the pistons, valve heads, spark plugs, and behind both compression rings. This carbon can build up to the point where the compression rings stick in their grooves and no longer press against the cylinder walls with enough pressure to seal the cylinder. Or it could go the other way, and not let the compression rings retract into the groove when they should, which can crack a ring, gouge a cylinder, and,

basically, screw up your engine's top end.

Piston rings are available in different materials, so they're better suited to their intended purpose, be it a fast break-in for racing, a slow one for longevity, or for use with ductile steel cylinders. Most rings are high-grade cast iron, ductile iron, or steel. What's best for your intended use is something you should discuss with your piston/cylinder supplier. In this book, we're going to only concern ourselves with the basics and the proper way to measure, fit, and install the little buggers.

Below the rings, on two sides of the piston, are the piston skirts, which drop down lower than the other two sides of the piston. The skirts are longer to help stabilize the piston in the cylinder as it pivots (rocks) on its wrist pin. The wrist pin

2. Spray the cylinder bores with WD-40 and wipe them out using clean rags. Keep spraying and wiping until the rag comes out clean, with no machining residue. Then do the same to all rings, wrist pins, and pistons.

3. Position each ring in the cylinder with the top of the piston so they're level in the bore and measure the gap with a flat feeler gauge. Follow the piston manufacturer specs concerning end gaps.

73

connects the piston to its connecting rod. The wrist pin, which is made of a hardened steel alloy that's precision ground, rides in the piston's thick, reinforced wrist pin holes. These holes are in the two sides of the piston that are not skirted. The wrist pin is a free-floating type in that it can move in its connecting rod bushing, as well as in the piston's wrist pin holes. Unlike cylinders and piston rings, pistons are not perfect circles. The sides with the wrist pin holes are narrower than the sides with the skirts. The piston's widest points are sometimes at the bottom end of the skirts, though most current piston designs are actually egg-shaped with their widest points in the middle of the skirts. Pistons also usually have some webbing on their underside for strength and to aid in cooling.

4. To increase a gap, use a good ring grinding tool and use the support pins on the tool to stabilize the ring you're working on. Take your time and grind the ring ends straight, no angled cuts allowed.

Pistons come in many different shapes and styles, depending on the type of engine they'll be operating in. On a stock Harley-Davidson 80-cubic-inch Evo engine, the piston skirts are long and do not have a notch cut into them for the connecting rod. Also, the piston ring grooves are above and away from the wrist pin holes. However, on a stroker (an engine with a longer-than-stock stroke), this may not be the case. One of the piston skirts, the one that the connecting rod swings near when moving through its arc, may be shorter or have a notch cut into it to give the connecting rod the room it needs to pull the piston down farther in its cylinder. This modification may also be needed to keep the rear skirt of the front piston from hitting the front skirt of the rear piston at the bottom of the pistons' strokes. (Read Chapter 7: Stroking for more on this.) To keep the piston from slamming into the head as it travels farther up the cylinder due to the longer stroke, a piston in a stroked engine is not as tall as one in a stock stroke engine. In fact, on a very long stroke motor the piston may be so short that the oil ring groove actually cuts across the wrist pin holes. A piston made to fit a specific combustion chamber design may have an odd-shaped dome. One that has been clearanced for use with a high-lift cam may have very deep valve pockets cut into the top of the piston.

Motorcycle pistons are also made of different types of aluminum alloy, using different manufacturing processes. And though we're not going to recommend what piston type you should use with certain other performance parts, a brief discussion on what's currently available is definitely in order. At the bottom of the list is the cast piston. Cheap to produce and possessing decent strength, the cast piston is the choice of budget builders who are not constructing a high-performance and/or high-compression engine. A forged piston is much stronger than a cast one and it's a good choice for a performance engine. These pistons also come in different aluminum alloys. Some carry a T-6 heat treatment rating, which greatly increases piston strength. Another possible and excellent choice for a performance engine is a hypoeutectic piston. These are lighter than most forged pistons and have high-heat strength. They also have better shape retention than a conventional forged piston, so they can be installed with closer piston-to-cylinder clearances.

As mentioned in the introduction, this book was written for the mechanic who wants to build his own engines. However, boring and honing a cylinder are specialized tasks that require expensive and specialized equipment, such as cylinder torque plates and boring bars, to be done correctly. Don't try to do these processes yourself in the home garage with an electric drill and hone tool. A qualified engine shop, whether it's for autos or specifically for motorcycles (the better of the two), is the place to have this work done.

PREP WORK

Installing the pistons and cylinders, like the oil pump, is an easy process. Even the prep work, outside of the machining, is easy. Just take your time and check your measurements a few times before making any changes.

Check that the oil passages on the cylinders line up with the ones on the crankcase. Do this by laying the new gaskets against the parts in question and then the crankcase. If the holes in the part/crankcase line up with the holes in the gasket, you're all set. If not, find out why and correct the problem.

Check all threaded holes. Make sure they are free of debris and dirt. Make sure all threads are in good shape and will not strip out when you reinstall whatever goes into them at the correct torque. Now is the time to weld up, machine flat, drill, and rethread a stripped hole.

Check the condition of all the parts you plan on installing in this part of the build. Look for signs of scuffing or pitting on all components. Any grooves or scoring on the body of a piston, wrist pin, or in the bore of a cylinder is not

acceptable. If you can feel the mark with your fingernail, it's too deep to reuse if it's a piston. If it's a feel-able mark on a cylinder bore, the imperfection must be removed by boring and/or honing to the next oversize piston available for that particular bore size. Also check that all gasket surfaces are free of gouges, imprints, marks with depth, or any other imperfections that may allow oil to get past the gaskets.

When checking the piston-to-cylinder clearance, use a bore gauge to get the bore diameter. By the way, this clearance spec is set by the cylinder, and in some cases also the piston, manufacturer. This spec is not usually controlled by the size of the bore, like the piston ring end gap is. The determining factor here is the growth rate of the piston compared to the growth rate of the

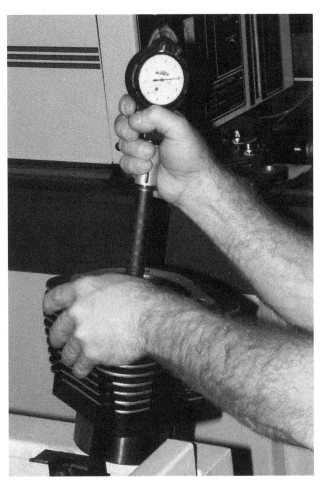

5. To check the piston-to-cylinder clearance, Reg uses a bore gauge to get the cylinder's bore diameter. On stock H-D sleeved aluminum cylinders, you want 0.00075"- 0.00175".

75

6. Measure the piston at the points determined by the manufacturer to get the full diameter of the piston. Unlike cylinders and piston rings, pistons are not perfect circles.

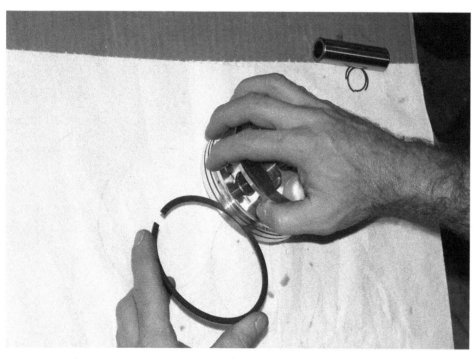

7. Next, poke a ring into its groove backwards and make sure it can go into the groove about 0.006" below the outer edge. Check each ring in its own groove and don't mix up the rings and pistons.

cylinder as they both heat up to operating temperature. Each component's growth rate is determined by the material it's made of. For example, a common forged piston will require more clearance than a cast one since the forged piston will grow (expand) faster than the cast one. In a ductile iron big-bore cylinder, the forged aluminum piston will require even more clearance since it will grow much faster than the bore of the ductile iron cylinder. And since pistons don't move very well in their cylinder when they're bigger than the hole they're in, this is a very important clearance to get right. The bottom line is to go with the cylinder and piston supplier's specs. If you're not using a matched set from one manufacturer, follow both the cylinder and piston manufacturer's spec. If in doubt, call them both and ask their recommendations. Be sure to do this before you end gap the piston rings, since the end gaps will be wrong if you have to open up the cylinder bore a bit more.

Check the fit of all the parts you plan on assembling for this section of the build, whether old or new. Do this with the parts at room temperature, not cold or hot. After cleaning the wrist pins, check each one's fit in its piston. If they're past the manufacturer's specs, replace it. For me, unless the wrist pin has only a few thousand miles on it, I never reuse an old one. You always get a new wrist pin with a new piston. As for the wrist pin's fit in its connecting rod bushing, if you haven't already done this in Chapter 1, H-D's spec is loose: 0.0003"-0.0007". H-D calls for replacement of the bushing and/or pin, depending on which is at fault, if it exceeds 0.001". For H-D, the proper fit of a new wrist pin in its piston is loose: 0.0001"-0.0004". If you're using a different manufacturer's piston, go by their specs.

As for the proper fitment of the rings on the piston, rings in the cylinder, and piston in the cylinder, we'll be checking these as part of the assembly process. At this point, just make sure the chamfer at the bottom of each cylinder has a decent taper to it, so the piston rings can be easily walked into the cylinder bore when the time comes.

Since pistons and cylinders, like all moving parts, wear, pistons come in different oversizes. For Evo-style engines, H-D and a number of other piston suppliers offer oversized pistons in various sizes starting with 0.005" and ending with 0.030" for a standard H-D Evolution cylinder. If you're using a different manufacturer's cylinder, follow their guidelines on acceptable overbores, and piston and ring fitment specs. Harley-Davidson requires piston replacement to the next oversize when the piston-to-cylinder clearance exceeds 0.003". Piston replacement is also needed

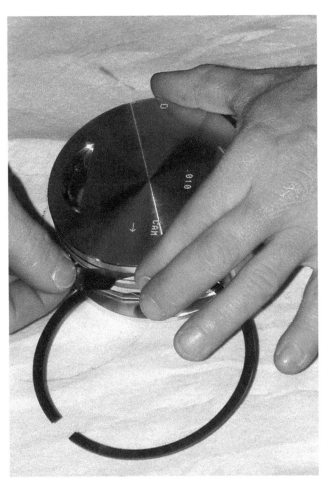

8. Lastly, use a flat feeler gauge to check the side clearance of each ring in its groove to make sure it's at least 0.002". H-D spec for the top ring is 0.002"-0.0045" and 0.0016"- 0.0041" for the second.

9. Install one wrist pin clip into its groove in the piston using the proper tool or your fingers, depending on the clip's design. Then put new cylinder base gaskets onto the crankcases.

if a compression ring's side clearance in its groove exceeds 0.006" or an oil ring's side clearance is beyond 0.008". As for piston rings, the next oversize is needed when compression ring end gap exceeds 0.030" or the oil control rings end gap exceeds 0.065" as per H-D spec.

The cylinder must also be checked. The bore of the cylinder must not be tapered. If you detect a difference of 0.002" between the top of the bore and any other section, the cylinder must be bored true again and fitted with new pistons. The same holds true if the cylinder is out of round by more than 0.003" at any point in the length of the bore. Also check both gasket surfaces for warping. H-D states that the head gasket surface variation cannot exceed 0.006", while the cylinder base must not be more than 0.008". (If you have

more, read the section on head decking in Chapter 5: The Heads.)

If you're reusing the stock H-D aluminum cylinders, check that the steel sleeve is not separating from the aluminum finned casting at any point. If it is, replace the cylinder. A common location for this separation is at the top of the cylinder, where the steel sleeve joins the aluminum casting. See if you can slip a 0.002" flat feeler gauge into the gap between the two. Sometimes the steel liner is actually protruding slightly higher than the aluminum gasket surface. Run your fingernail inward from the gasket surface to the steel liner to see if you can feel the liner. Cylinder replacement is the only fix for either of these cylinder flaws.

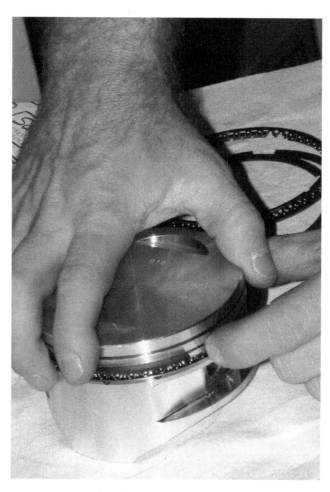

10. Install the rings onto their piston, as per the piston manufacturer's specs. Start with the three-piece oil ring set. The first part of this set to go on is the ridged expander.

11. The second and top compression rings go on next, in that order, noting the piston manufacturer's orientation marks. Sometimes it's a bevel that goes up, sometimes it's a dot.

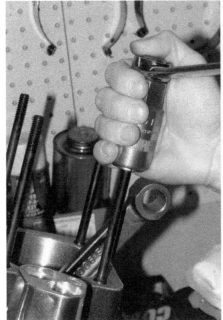  

12. With red Loctite on the new cylinder studs, install the studs using an installation tool as per the instructions. (Never reuse an old stud.) Then cover the studs with sections of rubber hose to protect the pistons and rings.

13. Once the wrist pin bore is lubed, slip the pin into its hole only as far as the gap in the piston for the rod. Then position the piston over its connecting rod, and send the pin the rest of the way through.

14. With clean rags in the spigot holes, pop in the last wrist pin clip just like the first one. Remember to position the one end of the clip over the clip-removal notch on the piston's wrist pin hole.

ASSEMBLY TIPS

The accompanying photos and captions cover two complete assembly procedures. The first is for a standard cylinder stud-style engine, like you find on a stock H-D Evo, and pistons that use wrist pin clips. The other is for a base stud-style engine, which is the version some builders prefer to use with a very big-bore or high-horsepower engine. This is because very high horsepower outputs can make cylinder studs rock as the engine goes through its power pulses. In time, the cylinder studs pull out from the crankcases, making quite a mess of your engine. These engines are usually also fitted with pistons with wrist pin buttons instead of clips, since very high power outputs are also known for popping out wrist pin clips. A loose clip will destroy a cylinder wall in no time. We're using one of R&R Cycle's big-inch beauties for the base stud sequence.

As for the two sequences, though you will note many similarities between them, there are important differences. So you don't skip a step or miss a check that may cause an engine failure, I've given you both as two complete and separate sequences. While some may think I'm wasting space, I believe it's much more important that you have a series of steps that you can follow, from start to finish, that are specific for your style of engine and piston so you don't make an expensive mistake.

Though the captions explain in detail what the photo is showing you, here are several more tips and bits of info that'll make the job go easier and/or help you avoid expensive mistakes. These apply to both cylinder stud-style engines and base nut-style ones.

When checking the end gap on the piston rings, use a piston turned upside down to push each ring down into the cylinder bore evenly so you get a correct end gap measurement. If the ring is cocked or crooked in the cylinder you'll get a false reading. If the gap is too small, the ends of the rings will butt against each other when the engine reaches operating temperature. This will cause the ring to break, scoring the cylinder and ruining both it and the piston. Too large a gap brings you close (or past) the rebuild spec even though the engine is new.

Check the ring manufacturer's instructions on how to tell which ring is the top compression ring and which is the second, if they are different. Also check to see if one side of the ring is designed to face up when installed on the piston. There may be a dot or taper on the ring that must be positioned either up or down for proper ring operation. Once you fit a ring to a piston and cylinder, make sure you keep them together as a set. By that, I mean once you end gap a set of rings to

the front cylinder, make sure those rings are installed onto the front piston. As a rule don't mix up rings, pistons, and cylinders after you've fitted them. Sometimes it doesn't matter, but if you get in the habit of always keeping them separate you can't get yourself in trouble.

If you have to increase a ring's end gap, take your time and grind the ring ends straight. No angled cuts allowed. Do a little grinding and then check the gap again. Once you have the correct gap, wipe the ring down with WD-40 and a clean rag to get all metal filings off.

There are three reasons to hone a cylinder. The first is to size it to the new piston. The second is for oil retention. The third is to give the new rings a rough surface to rub against and mate

15. Put assembly lube on the wrist pin bore and piston skirt under the oil rings and oil the cylinder bore. But keep the rings and ring lands clean of oil or lube. Lube and install the ring compressor. Remove rubber hoses.

16. Position the cylinder over and on top of its piston. Gently walk the cylinder over the piston. Then remove the ring compressor, followed by the rag in the spigot hole. Now tap the cylinder onto the cases.

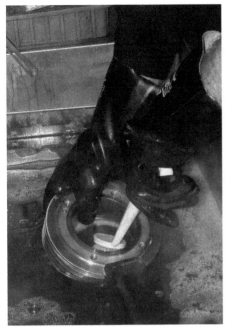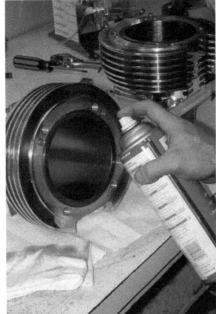

Assembly Sequence #2
1. Once the cylinders have been machined, thoroughly wash them with hot water and soap, including all oil passageways. Then rinse with fresh water and blow them clean and dry with compressed air.

2. Spray the cylinder bores with WD-40 and wipe them out using clean rags. Keep spraying and wiping until the rag comes out clean, with no machining residue. Then do the same to all rings, wrist pins, and pistons.

3. Position each ring in the cylinder with the top of the piston so they're level in the bore and check the end gap with a flat feeler gauge. Follow the piston manufacturer's specs concerning end gaps.

to. Rings do not, should not, move on the piston once they're broken in, unlike a valve, which does move on its seat in the head. In fact, an improper crosshatch pattern or too fine a hone, one that does not give the rings a rough enough surface to seat to, can result in insufficient oil retention and cause the piston to seize in the cylinder. There can also be oil consumption problems. For these reasons, never reinstall used rings.

When installing a piston onto a connecting rod, besides making sure you have the front piston going onto the front rod if there is a difference between them, you must also note whatever marker denotes the front of the piston. Sometimes, as you can see on the top of the piston in photo 8 of the first assembly sequence, there's an arrow imprinted on the piston's dome. This arrow must be aimed as per the manufacturer's guidelines. Some arrows are to face the front of the engine, on both the front and rear pistons.

Others will face the exhaust ports, which means the arrow on the front piston faces the front of the engine while the arrow on the rear piston faces to the rear. On a stroker engine, the short skirt or skirt with the notch is the telltale marker. On the front piston, this short skirt/notch goes on the rear of the piston, so the piston can clear the connecting rod and the front skirt of the rear piston at the bottom of its stroke. On the rear piston, the short skirt/notch is at the front of the piston, again, to give clearance for the connecting rod and rear skirt of the front piston. Some piston manufacturers only shorten/notch the front of the rear piston for Bottom Dead Center (BDC) clearance.

Another indicator is the two notches cut in the piston's dome for the valves. The larger, wider, deeper, of the two is for the intake valve, since it's always the larger of the two valves. The intake valve notch (relief) helps you properly position

4. To increase an end gap, use a good ring grinding tool and use the support pins on the tool to stabilize the ring you're working on. Take your time and grind the ring ends straight, no angled cuts allowed.

5. To check the piston-to-cylinder clearance, use a bore gauge to get the cylinder's bore diameter. This clearance spec is set by the cylinder, and sometimes also the piston, manufacturer.

the piston. On the front cylinder, the intake valve relief is on the rear of the piston dome, since that's where the intake valve is in the head. On the rear cylinder, it's on the front of the piston dome.

While we're on the subject of valve reliefs, if you're installing a high-lift cam, larger valves, or a set of domed higher compression pistons, you must check for proper clearance between the valves and the piston dome. This is done with the cylinders on and when you're working on the heads. How to do this is described in Chapter 7: Special Procedures under the heading Claying The Pistons.

When installing each wrist pin clip into its groove in the piston (if used), use the proper tool or your fingers, depending on the clip's design. For the clip style shown in photo 9 of the Cylinder Stud-Style Engines sequence, insert the clip as shown and use your fingers to push the clip deeper into the hole, which squeezes the clip to the right size. Then push the top of the clip into its groove in the piston wrist pin hole. When installing the wrist pin clips into their grooves in the piston, Reg recommends positioning one end of the clip over the piston's clip removal hole, as shown in photo 14 of the Cylinder Stud-Style Engines assembly sequence. This makes it easier to remove the clips when it's time for the next rebuild. Install one wrist pin clip into the piston before installing the piston onto its connecting rod.

As for the wrist pins, after the wrist pin bore is lubed, slip the wrist pin into the piston's wrist pin hole, but only as far as the gap in the piston for the connecting rod. Then position the piston over its connecting rod, noting whatever marker denotes the front of the piston, and send the wrist pin the rest of the way through. Stop the pin just before it touches the wrist pin clip already installed.

When installing the oil rings onto their piston, if the expander doesn't fit the piston (the ends overlap), you probably have the wrong size rings for that piston size. As explained, rings, like pistons, come in oversizes. And no, you can't alter the oil rings to fit. A piston ring must be a perfect circle that matches the arc of its cylinder's bore. If the rings are not the right ones for that size cylinder bore, though you can grind the ends for the correct end gap, the arc of the ring will be wrong, so it will not seal correctly to the cylinder's bore. Oil will then get past the rings and into the combustion chamber, causing the problems mentioned earlier. Compression will also leak past the compression rings and pressurize the lower end, resulting in oil blow-by out of the engine's breathers. The engine will also run poorly.

When installing the rings onto their piston, start with the three-piece oil ring set. The first part of this set to go on is the ridged expander,

followed by the lower oil ring and then the upper oil ring. The second and top compression rings go on next, in that order, noting the piston manufacturer's orientation marks. Sometimes the orientation mark is a bevel that goes up, sometimes it's a dot. Installing rings upside down, if they have a special cut to them, will result in a poor seal to the cylinder, and oil and compression blow-by issues.

You also get oil and compression blow-by problems if you screw up the spacing of the ring gaps. The Harley-Davidson service manual for an early 1990s Evo calls for the ring end gaps to be placed in these specific locations: If you look at the top of the piston and consider it the face of a conventional clock, the front of the piston is at the 12 o'clock position. The top compression

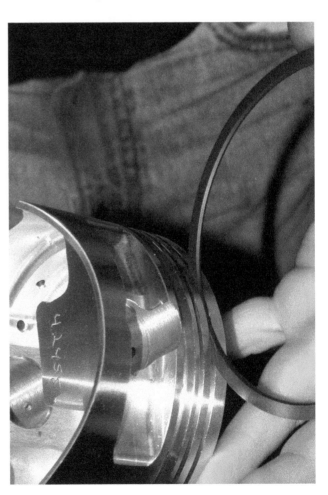

6. Measure the piston at the points determined by the manufacturer to get the full diameter of the piston. Unlike cylinders and piston rings, pistons are not perfect circles.

7. Next, poke a ring into its groove backwards and make sure it can go into the groove about 0.006" below the outer edge. Check each ring in its own groove and don't mix up the rings and pistons.

ring's gap goes between the 4 and 5 o'clock spots. The second compression ring's gap goes between the 10 and 11 o'clock positions. As for the oil ring gaps, one goes between the 7 and 8 o'clock spots, while the other one goes directly opposite it, between 1 and 2 o'clock. The oil ring expander's gap is to be placed at the same position as the top compression ring's gap. H-D wants you to position the rings gaps in these same positions for both the front and rear pistons.

Some mechanics use the just described H-D pattern, with a twist. Since the area of the piston dome by the exhaust valve is the hottest part of the piston, they only use the H-D pattern for the front piston. This puts the front piston's top compression ring gap (and, therefore, its two ring

ends) near the much cooler intake valve. On the rear piston, they flip the H-D pattern, making the rear of the piston the 12 o'clock spot. This puts the top compression ring next to the rear head's intake valve, between the H-D 10 and 11 o'clock position, with the second ring gap between the H-D 4 and 5 o'clock, etc.

Reg prefers to use a different pattern on his very large displacement engines. Again, looking at the top of the front piston so the front is at 12 o'clock, he places the top compression ring's gap at 4 o'clock, while the second compression ring is at 8 o'clock. The gaps for the oil control rings go between 1 and 2 o'clock and 10 and 11 o'clock. He places the oil expander ring at 12 o'clock. On the rear piston, with the front of the piston at 12

8. For the last piston-to-ring check, Reg uses a flat feeler gauge to check the side clearance of each ring in its groove to ensure it's at least 0.002". New cylinder base gaskets are then put onto the crankcases.

9. Install the rings onto their piston as per the piston manufacturer's specs. The expander of the three-piece oil ring set goes on first, followed by the lower oil ring and then the upper oil ring.

o'clock, he places the top compression ring's gap at 2 o'clock, while the second compression ring is at 10 o'clock. The gaps for the oil control rings go between 4 and 5 o'clock and 7 and 8 o'clock. He places the oil expander ring at 6 o'clock.

When it's time to install the cylinder, make sure the cylinder's base gaskets are on the crankcases. Then lightly lube the piston skirt under the oil rings with assembly lube and the cylinder bore with motor oil. However, keep the rings and ring lands clean of oil or lube. You don't want to load the ring lands with oil/lube that will turn to carbon when the engine fires off. Put the proper size piston ring compressor tool, with just a skin coat of oil on its inner face (the section that will touch the rings), over the piston. The top of

the tool should be slightly below the top of the piston, but covering the top ring. Then remove the rubber hoses from the studs. Position the cylinder over and on top of its piston, supporting its weight with one hand, while you hold the piston in position with the ring compressor. Gently walk the cylinder from side to side, wrist pin hole to wrist pin hole, with your supporting hand to get the top ring to enter into the cylinder. Once the cylinder is over the top ring, gently tap the top of the cylinder over one wrist pin hole and then the other to rock the cylinder a little from side to side. This will walk the rest of the rings into the cylinder bore without cracking a ring. However, you must watch as the rings enter the cylinder bore to make sure one edge hasn't

10. Install the second compression ring onto the piston as per the piston manufacturer's specs. Then do the same for the top ring. Next, position the piston ring end gaps.

11. Put assembly lube on the wrist pin bore and piston skirt under the oil rings and oil the cylinder bore. But keep the rings and ring lands clean of oil or lube.

popped out from under the ring compressor and is jammed against the edge of the cylinder bore. If this happens, try to push the ring back into its groove in the piston and into the cylinder bore with your fingernail or a piece of plastic, not a metal tool like a screwdriver. Then remove the ring compressor, followed by the rag you put in the cylinder spigot hole, and tap the cylinder all the way down onto the crankcases.

R&R Cycle uses a specific torque sequence to secure its base-stud cylinders to the crankcases, which I believe is a good system to follow on any similar cylinder-to-crankcase setup, like on a high performance Shovelhead. In a cross pattern, Reg does all four nuts to 10 ft-lbs., then 20, then 30, and ends with a final torque of 45 ft-lbs. As you

do this, make sure the cylinder does not shift to one (the down) side of the stud holes. The cylinder studs must stay in the center of the cylinder stud holes as you tighten down the nuts.

WEEPING CYLINDER GASKETS

For the entire 1984-99 production cycle of the Evo Big Twins there's been a problem with oil weeping from the cylinder base gaskets. All during that time, the factory tried various gasket fixes to no avail. And though the factory even tried Kevlar gaskets, the problem persisted since the gaskets are not the problem. The problem is the design of the cylinder-to-crankcase oil return system.

There are two easy ways to fix this annoying problem. The first is the Hayden Oil-Fix, which comes with two dowels and new base gaskets. To

12. With the wrist pin halfway in its piston and lube in the connecting rod bore, position each piston onto its rod, noting proper orientation. This big-bore engine uses Teflon wrist pin buttons instead of clips.

13. With the piston in a ring compressor with a skin coat of oil on it, position the cylinder over the piston. Gently tap the cylinder down over the piston with your hand, so the rings slip into the cylinder. Then remove the rag in the spigot.

install the kit, simply press the large end of one of the dowels into the front oil return hole on the front cylinder and the other dowel into the rear oil return hole on the rear cylinder. The small end of each dowel fits into the oil drain holes of the crankcases. Then reinstall the top end with the new base gaskets. The dowels channel oil directly from the cylinders into the crankcases and keep it away from the base gaskets. The kit is available from Hayden and a number of other vendors for $40-$48.

The second fix, installing a Base Gasket By-Pass Pigtail Kit, requires a minor alteration to the cylinder and is available from Fog Hollow and other vendors for $50-$60. To install the kit, tap the front oil return hole on the front cylinder and the rear oil return hole on the rear cylinder with the kit's supplied aluminum tap. Then screw one of the kit's Pigtail tubes into the just-tapped holes so about an inch of the tube is protruding down and into its mating oil return hole in the crankcase. Like the Hayden fix, this modification keeps the return oil away from the cylinder base gaskets. According to the kit's instructions, this setup works best with metal base gaskets and fits all stock size Big Twin and Sportster cylinders. Simply pick the kit you're more comfortable with, but definitely do something to fix this design flaw during your rebuild.

COMPUTING DISPLACEMENT

Want to know an engine's displacement? One formula you can use to compute the displacement of a cylinder is: pi/4 x Bore x Bore x Stroke = Cylinder Displacement. The value pi is a number needed to find the area of a circle and is commonly used as 3.1416. The bore is the diameter of the cylinder. The stroke is how far the piston travels from Bottom Dead Center (BDC) to Top Dead Center (TDC). (Check out Chapter 1: The Bottom End for more on this.)

If we use the measurements of a standard 107-cubic-inch engine, which has a 4" bore and a 4-1/4" stroke, the formula would look like this: 3.1416 (pi)/4 x 4 (bore) x 4 (bore) x 4-1/4 (stroke) = 53.407 (half of the two-cylinder engine's displacement). To get the engine's total displacement, just multiply the displacement of one cylinder by the number of cylinders the engine has, which, in this case, is two: 53.407 x 2 = 106.814 or 107 cubic inches.

14. Once the cylinder is on the crankcases, tighten down the cylinder base nuts in a crisscross pattern. Check with the manufacturer of your cylinders to see what torque sequence they require.

Chapter Five

The Heads

Out with the bad air, in with the good

The heads on an engine do two things. First, they form the top fixed wall to our combustion chamber so we can get useful work from the combustion event. Second, they're fitted with the means of getting a fresh air/fuel charge into the cylinder for burning and then getting the waste gases, what's left over after the combustion event, out. How quickly the head can do its second task without failing at the first is what headwork is all about.

Truth is, it's not how high the cam lift is, or how big the carb is, or how loud the pipes are, or any of the other things some people brag about

The stock Evo head (right) has a D-shaped combustion chamber, while the R&R billet head has a bathtub-shaped chamber like a Twin Cam. The bathtub shape gives you two squish areas, while the D-shaped head only has one.

All 1984-92 Evo heads have a blind threaded hole on the upper corner for the air cleaner mounting bracket bolts. Don't confuse this with the breather bolt hole found on 1993-99 heads.

SPECIAL TOOL LIST	
Stiff bristle bottle brushes	40-ounce hammer
Parts cleaning tank	Rubber-tipped valve lapping tool
Compressed air supply	Valve spring height gauge
Clean shop cloths	Bench vise
Gauge block (or spring pressure tool and flat feeler gauge)	Valve check tool
	Flat feeler gauge
	Fine tooth file
Micrometer	Spring pressure tool
Dial ball gauge (or plain ball gauge)	0.060"-thick wire
	0.080"-thick wire
Torque wrench (in-lbs.)	Valve spring tester
	Valve seal installer
Torque wrench (ft-lbs.)	Plastic valve seal protector
Valve lapping compound (280- to 400-grit)	Valve spring compressor
	Blue Loctite
Assembly lube	Red Loctite
Valve guide installer	Motor oil
	Black marker

when claiming their bike is fast. The only factors that have anything to do with making power are getting the most air/fuel mixture over the piston as possible, mixing that mixture as perfectly as possible, and igniting it at just the right time to get the most useful work out of the pressure that's the result of the expansion of the hot gases of combustion. Power, actually torque, is created by changing chemical energy into heat energy and then into mechanical energy. Want more power? Efficiently burn more air (actually oxygen) and fuel over the top of the piston! It's as simple as that. Porting heads, installing bigger valves, increasing displacement, high-performance cams, etc. are all designed to burn more air/fuel mixture over the piston. Period!

What the accompanying assembly photos and captions are going to show you is how to properly assemble a set of Evo heads, starting with a stripped head and working all the way through to installing them on the engine. These photos will also show you how to check every clearance and tolerance needed when installing a set of performance valve

On 1993-99 Evos, the pressurized air that must be vented from the lower end is allowed to leave the engine and enter into the air cleaner housing via a 1/2" port in the upper corner of each head.

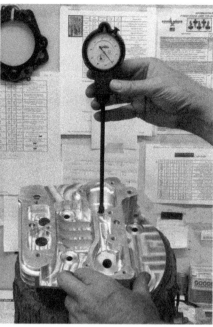

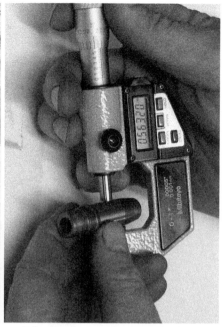

1. We start with a stripped head that has its oil passages and threaded holes checked and cleaned. Head was then washed using a cleaning tank, stiff bristle bottle brushes, and compressed air.

2. First in are the new valve guides. Check inner diameter (ID) of the guide hole using a dial bore gauge, or ball gauge and micrometer. Do this for each hole and write down the sizes and locations for present and future reference.

3. Then measure the outside diameter (OD) of each guide using a dial micrometer, write down the sizes, and compare each guide to its hole. You want a 0.002" - 0.003" press (interference) fit between the head and guide.

springs. These special springs and collars are a necessity when installing a performance camshaft if the cam has more lift than the stock one. They're also needed if the engine will be spun (revved) past the safe limit for the stock valve springs. However, don't make a common novice mistake and install the strongest (highest pressure) springs you can buy. The higher the valve spring pressure, the more wear on the valves and seats, as well as the rest of the valvetrain. Use the lightest springs the cam manufacturer requires and you'll be good to go.

CAM LIFT & VALVE LIFT

Many a novice mechanic has confused cam lift and valve lift. I know I did. Cam lift is measured from a point on the cam's base circle to the highest point, which is the centerline of the elliptically shaped cam lobe. The exact spot on the cam lobe used as the starting place for our measurements is usually the point where the cam's lobe has increased in height 0.053" higher (some cam manufacturers start at 0.20" and are listed as such) than the lowest

point on the base circle. Since we can take a measurement right on the actual cam lobe, without any variables such as lash between moving parts getting in the way, cam lift can be measured very precisely.

Valve lift is how far the valve actually leaves its valve seat. Valve lift can not be measured as accurately as cam lift because of variables in the valvetrain, like valve angles, pushrod length, pushrod angularity, lash between parts, and the exact ratio of the rocker's arms (which may vary a few thousands-of-an-inch due to manufacturing tolerances). Valve lift is measured using the valvetrain, but without the rocker box cover on, so a dial indicator can be setup on the valve stem to measure the actual amount the valve opens.

Valve lift will always be greater than the engine's cam lift on all H-D Big Twins except the Knucklehead. This is because the arms of the rockers used on all H-D Big Twins since the 1948 Panhead are not on the same plane. The pushrod-actuated arm of the rocker is closer to the rocker's

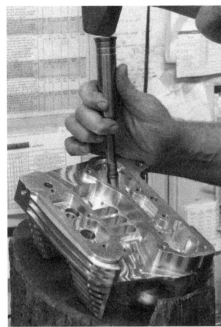

4. Install the guides into their holes using a valve guide installer, green Loctite, and 40-ounce hammer. Drive the guide fully against the head. You'll feel a change in how the hammer strikes the guide when the guide is seated.

5. Check the fit of each valve in its guide using a gauge block or micrometer to find the OD of the valve stem. Write this number down for each valve for present and future reference.

6. Use a dial bore gauge to measure the guide's ID. You usually want 0.0015" - 0.002" of clearance for an intake valve and 0.002" - 0.0025" for an exhaust in a typical installation, but check with the valve manufacturer for your build.

pivot point than the valve-actuating arm, which results in an increase in lift at the valve. The 1936-47 Knuckleheads have their rockers' arms at the same height in relation to the pivot point, so it is said to have a 1:1 ratio. Since the Knuckle's rocker arms have no offset, the cam lift and valve lift are (theoretically) equal. Panheads have a 1.50:1 rocker ratio. The 1966-69 kidney-shaped cam cover Shovelheads can use the same cams as the cone cam cover Shovelheads, since they both have a rocker arm ratio of 1.42:1. Evo and Twin Cam rocker arms also have the same ratio: 1.625:1.

CHANGES

The only major change made to the H-D Evo heads was due to the conversion from a crankcase breather system contained in the gearcase section and right crankcase to a head breather system in 1993. On 1984-92 Evo engines, the pressurized oily air from the bottom end goes through a set of baffles in the cam cover (this setup is shown in Chapter 3: The Gearcase) to separate as much oil

from the pressurized air as possible before the air is vented to the atmosphere through a fitting in the right crankcase, located just inboard and below the oil pump. A hose connects this fitting to the air cleaner housing, so the pressurized air from the engine can be sucked into the engine and burned during the combustion event. On 1993-99 Evo models, the routing of the pressurized oily air now travels from the gearcase section, up the pushrod tubes, and into the middle section of each rocker box. Some oil separates from the pressurized air as it travels up the pushrod tubes. Once in the rocker boxes, the pressurized still-oily air passes through a filter that separates most or all of the oil from the air. This now-cleaner air then passes through the umbrella valve and into the air cleaner housing via a 1/2" port and hollow bolt in the right side of each head. Don't mistake the blind threaded hole for the air cleaner mounting bracket bolts that are in this same area on 1984-92 heads for breather bolt holes (ports). The breather bolt hole in the later-style

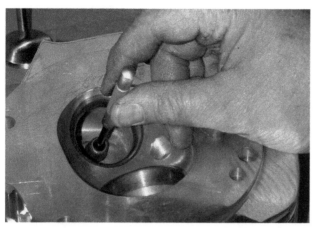

7. You can also use a plain ball gauge and micrometer to measure the inside diameter of the guide. Put the ball gauge in the middle of the guide and expand the gauge so it fills the bore (ID) of the guide.

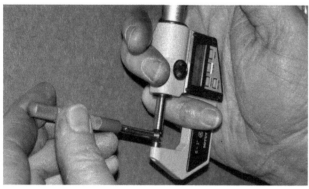

8. Then use a micrometer to measure the gauge's ball to get the guide's ID at that point. Also take measurements at both ends of the guide. If the measurements at all three locations are the same, the guide is straight. If not, reject the guide.

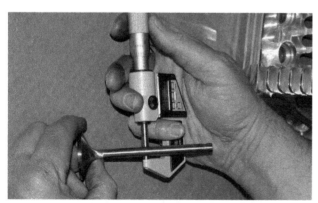

9. Then use a micrometer to measure the OD of the valve for that guide. Measure an exhaust valve in the middle, since these are slightly narrower near the head; measure intake valves anywhere along its stem.

1993-99 heads is larger and doesn't have a bottom. Once the pressurized air from the engine is in the air cleaner housing, it's sucked into the combustion chambers and burned during the combustion event.

PREP WORK

When you disassemble the engine, loosen the head bolts gradually, 1/8-turn at a time per head bolt in a cross pattern, so you don't warp the head, cylinder, or crankcase studs. When you disassemble the heads, make sure you note which valve the keepers were with and what head the valves were with if you plan on reusing the keepers and valves. An easy way to keep them sorted is to put them in plastic sandwich bags and label the bags with a black marker.

Start the reassembly by checking that all passageways in the heads are clean and clear of debris, be it metal filings, old carbon, dirt, or small bits of packing material if they are new heads. Use a stiff bristle bottlebrush, a cleaning tank, and some compressed air to clean out all passageways. The ones in the cylinders should have been checked and cleaned already as described in Chapter 4.

Check all threaded holes. Make sure they are free of debris and dirt. Make sure all threads are in good shape and will not strip out when you reinstall whatever goes into them at the correct torque. As with all the engine parts, now is the time to weld up, machine flat, drill, and rethread a stripped hole.

After spraying a shop cloth with brake clean, wipe off the gasket surfaces of the heads to remove any dirt or oily residue. Then check that all gasket surfaces are free of gouges, imprints, marks with depth (if you can feel it with your fingernail, it's too deep), or any other imperfections that may allow oil or cylinder pressure to get past the gaskets. Also check all four valve guide bores for gouges, scouring marks with depth, or any other imperfections that may cause an oil problem; replace any that are defective. Check the fit of all the keepers in their valve stem slots. Make sure the keys fit into their slot easily. If the key fits too tightly, replace them. Remove any burrs from the keepers or keeper slot on the valve stems with a very fine tooth file.

Check the head-to-cylinder gasket surface for

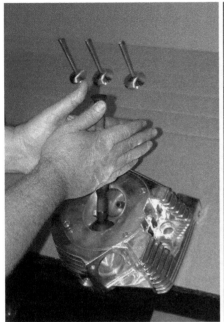

10. Assign each valve to a guide and mark it accordingly, as in FI for Front Intake, etc. Now lap the valves to their seats as per the process explained in Assembly Tips. Then thoroughly wash and dry the valves and heads again.

11. Check the spring pack's installed height using a spring height gauge or a micrometer as explained in Assembly Tips. Do all four valves and write down their specs for comparison against the valve spring's spec sheet. Our installed height is 1.810".

12. Next, install just the inner spring of the spring pack you plan on using, complete with the top and bottom spring collars and both spring keepers.

flatness and flaws. H-D states that the head gasket surface flatness cannot exceed 0.006". If yours is even just close to this limit, read the section on head decking, also called milling, in Chapter 7: Special Procedures. If the engine had oil consumption problems (smoking, oily slime build-up in the exhaust, etc.) before it was disassembled, also check for head casting porosity, as cautioned in H-D's 1993-94 Service Manual for FX/Softail Models (#99482-94), page 3-12.

Check that the oil passages in the head line up with the ones on the cylinders and lower rocker boxes. Do this by laying the new gaskets against the parts in question and then the head. If the holes in both parts line up with the holes in the gasket, you're all set. If not, find out why and correct the problem. Hopefully, you just have the wrong gasket.

Check the condition of all the parts you plan on installing in this part of the build. If you plan on reusing old parts, you must check all clearances as

per the engine manufacturer's specifications. If you're going to reuse the valves, glass-bead all carbon and other deposits from the valves before inspecting them. However, you should also check all clearances if you're using new components. How to do this is covered in this chapter's assembly photos and captions. Look for signs of scuffing or pitting on all components. Any grooves or scoring on the valve stem or a burned section on the valve head is cause for replacement. Do the same for all keepers, collars, shims, and valve springs.

Measure the valves and guides to make sure they are within useable specs. Check the length and pressure of the used valve springs to ensure they're still within spec before reusing them. The term interference fit is used at certain points of the inspection, fitment checks, and assembly process in the accompanying assembly sequence. An interference fit is when one part, like a valve guide, is slightly larger than the hole it will go into. The specs given in the captions are R&R's. The H-D specs, as listed in the 1993-94 Service Manual for FX/Softail Models, are as follows: The valve guide should be 0.0020" - 0.0033" larger than its hole in the head. If it's not, go to the next oversize guide. The valve seat in the head should be 0.0045" - 0.0020". The exhaust valve in its guide should be 0.0015" - 0.0033". If it exceeds 0.0040" with seal, the worn part should be replaced. The intake valve in

14. Check the valve-to-valve clearance using a flat feeler gauge: You need at least 0.060" or 0.080" for a high-performance engine. Got a high-lift cam? Check for valve-to-piston clearance at this time as per Claying The Pistons in Chapter 7.

13. Check valve-to-valve clearance with a valve check tool. Install the tool, position the arms, zero out both dial indicators, and turn the extenders to push down on the valve stems to the cam's Valve Lift At TDC spec.

its guide should be 0.0008" - 0.0026". If it exceeds 0.0035" with seal, the worn part should be replaced. H-D wants valve stem protrusion from the head to be within 1.990" - 2.024". If it exceeds 2.034", the seat should be replaced. Specs for the valves are as follows: stem taper should not exceed 0.0015", stem-to-face eccentricity not to exceed 0.002" and head margin (variation) not to exceed 0.031". The valve should be replaced for any of these flaws. If a valve is questionable, it should be replaced. As for the valve springs, here are H-D's allowable tolerances: The outer spring (closed) should have a pressure of 72 - 92 pounds when it's 1.751" - 1.848" in length. The outer spring (open) should have a pressure of 183 - 207 pounds when it's 1.282" - 1.378" in length. The total free length should be 2.105" - 2.177". The inner spring (closed) should have a pressure of 38 - 49 pounds when it's 1.577" - 1.683" in length. The inner spring (open) should have a pressure of 98 - 112 pounds when it's 1.107" - 1.213" in length. The total free length should be 1.926" - 1.996".

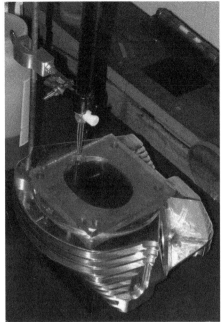  

15. Once the valve-to-valve and valve-to-piston clearances are set, it's time to check the volume of both combustion chambers. This process is detailed in Chapter 7: Special Procedures.

16. To check valve spring pressure, use a micrometer to measure top and bottom collars. Our top collar is 0.120", the bottom is 0.070", for a total of 0.190". Then assemble each spring pack with both collars and keep them as sets.

17. With a spring pack in a spring pressure testing tool, compress the pack to the installed spring height (1.810") plus the total of the collar measurements (0.190"). Then read the tool's pound dial to see what pressure the spring pack is at.

As stated earlier, these are the specs as per Harley's 1993-94 Service Manual for FX/Softail Models. The specs for your model and year H-D may be different. If you're rebuilding an S&S Cycle or other brand engine, they are probably different. Though the procedures and such will be the same, you should use your engine manufacturer's specs when rebuilding your engine.

ASSEMBLY TIPS

In the accompanying photos and captions, one of the staff of R&R Cycle does a complete fitment check and assembly procedure so you know how to do the job yourself, or how to check that the machine shop did the job to your specifications. R&R Cycle's owner Reggie Jr. then installs the heads onto the R&R 127-cubic-inch engine we've been building.

Once you've measured and checked a group of parts, keep them together as a set. Do not mix springs, collars, and valves. The same holds true if you're reusing old parts. They must go back into the same location as before. Don't mix them up.

When measuring the outside diameter (OD) of each guide and the inside diameter of each guide hole in the head you want a 0.002" - 0.003" press (interference) fit between the head and guide. If the guide is too small, go to whatever oversize guide necessary to get the interference fit needed. Guides usually come in oversizes that increase in increments of 0.001".

To lap each valve to its seat, put some 280- to 400-grit lapping compound on the head of the valve's seat, which is where it will contact the head's valve seat. Then insert the valve into its guide and let it contact its seat. Using a rubber-tipped valve tool, rotate the valve back and forth on its seat to cut both the valve's and head's seats until they're a perfectly matched set. The valve always rotates in its guide when the engine is running, so the seat must be tight for its full 360 degrees. Both seats are done when their color is uniform for the same width and the complete circle of both the valve and seat.

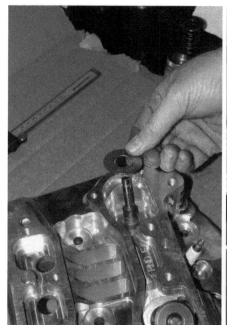  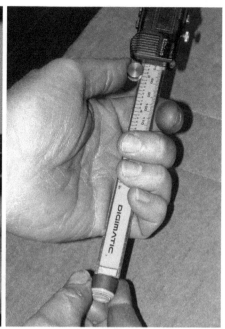

18. *If the spring pressure is higher than the spec in the cam's sheet, it depends on how much higher. If the pressure is lower, put some shims under the lower collar to increase it. Do this for all the spring packs.*

19. *Compress each spring until the spring is coil bound. Measure how far the spring is compressed (ours was 1.200") and check this against the spring's spec sheet Coil Bind Height number.*

20. *Measure the inside depth of the valve seals using a dial indicator (ours are 0.370") and measure the outside length (ours are 0.510"). Subtract the inside depth from the outside length. The difference (0.140") is subtracted from the next measurement.*

However, the seat in the head will not be the full width of the seat on the valve's head. Harley calls for, as per its 1993-94 Service Manual for FX/Softail Models, a seat width of 0.040" - 0.062". You're looking for a consistent width for the full circle of the seat on both the head and valve. After you've done all four valves, thoroughly wash and dry the heads and valves again.

To check a spring's installed height, install the valve in its guide and drop on the lower valve spring collar you intend to use. Then slip the valve spring height gauge over the valve stem and guide until it rests on the head. Then position the top valve spring collar onto the stem, followed by the two valve stem keepers (also called clips or keys). Now extend the spring height gauge fully until the tool is tight against the top collar. Then read the tool just like you would a micrometer, which you can also use to measure this. Do this for all four valves and write these numbers down for comparison against the camshaft's and valve spring's spec sheet. The

spring's installed height for ours is 1.810". If we're using a camshaft that has a lift at the valve of .560" (get this info from the cam's spec sheet), subtract the lift (0.560") from the spring height (1.810") and you get 1.250", which is what the spring height will be when the valve is fully open. The spring must be able to be compressed that much, plus 0.060" of safety clearance (subtract this from 1.250"), or 1.190". Use this number as the maximum Coil Bind Height (remember, less is better), which is listed on a performance valve spring set's spec sheet, when looking for an appropriate spring pack.

If you're using stock H-D heads, you can do a simple calculation to see if there may be a valve-to-valve clearance problem. Of course, the better way is to actually make the measurement using a valve checking tool. To use this tool, bolt the tool to the head and set the arms so they lay across the top of the upper valve collars. Then zero out both dial indicators and screw down the extenders so they push down on the valve stems to the Valve Lift At TDC spec listed on the camshaft's spec sheet. You can also measure the valve-to-valve clearance through the spark plug hole with a piece of 0.060"-thick wire (the old way). Here's how you do it: Check the spec sheet for the camshaft you're going to use. Find The Valve Lift At TDC spec and write it down. For this example, let's use the spec for a popular Andrews Evo cam, the EV59, which is .236". (The complete specs for this cam are given elsewhere in this chapter.) Now add to that the usual minimum safety clearance of 0.060" for a normal engine, which gives you 0.296". With both valves on their seats in the head, measure the distance between the valves at their closest points. The actual distance must be at least 0.296" (I'd round it up to 0.300"). However, if you're building a high-performance engine, 0.080" is what you want as a minimum safety clearance here, which would bring the minimum distance between the valves up to 0.316". If you don't have this much gap, you'll have to make the needed changes to make it so, such as cutting the valve seats deeper in the head or back-cutting the valves.

To check valve spring pressure, first measure the depth of the top collar at the first step using a micrometer. Then measure the bottom collar in the same way. Our top collar is 0.120", while our bottom is 0.070", for a total of 0.190". Now assemble each spring pack using both retaining collars and the inner and outer springs. From this point on, keep the retainers with the springs as a set, don't mix them up. After you've assembled each spring pack with its retainers, put the assembled spring

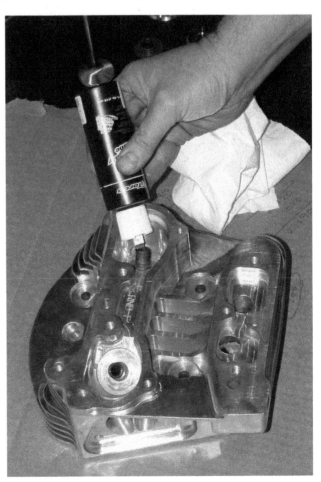

21. With a valve in its guide with its top collar and keepers, measure from the top of the guide to the inside face of the lowest section of the collar. Then subtract the seal measurement from step 20 to get the seal-to-collar clearance.

22. After the head has been thoroughly cleaned and dried, put assembly lube into the valve guides and onto the stem each valve. Then put each valve into its guide and move it around to spread the lube throughout the guide.

pack in a spring pressure testing tool. Adding the installed spring height (we got 1.810") to the total of the collar measurements (ours was 0.190") gives us the distance (2.000") we need to compress the spring pack on the spring pressure tool. As you compress the spring pack read the tool's pound dial to see what pressure the spring pack is at when compressed as it will be in the engine. If the spring pressure is higher than what's call for in the cam's spec sheet, how much higher determines if it's a problem. If the specs call for a minimum of 160, but the spring reads 180, that's okay. However, if it's more than 40 pounds over, you should use a different set of springs, or call the cam manufacturer. If the spring pressure is lower than the cam's spec, you can put some shims under the lower collar to increase it. How many you use depends on how much more pressure you need. Compress the spring

until you get the pressure you need and note how much farther you had to squeeze the springs to get it. Then add the corresponding distance in shims and retest to make sure it does bring the pressure up to spec, but will not bring the spring to coil bind (we check this next) when compressed, plus the safety factor. Check and correct, if needed, each spring pack in this way.

To check for spring coil bind, put each spring into the spring pressure testing tool (you can also do this in a vise but be careful!) and compresses the spring until you cannot pull a piece of paper from between its coils. This is when the spring is coil bound. Note where the indicator is and measure how far the spring was compressed (ours was 1.200") when it became coil bound. The allowable distance is called out on the spring's spec sheet as Coil Bind Height.

23. Slip the valve into its guide, followed by any shims (if needed), as per step 18. The valve spring shim is marked as to which side is up, so don't put it on upside down. You can then install the lower collar.

24. Using a seal installer, a plastic seal protector, and a plastic hammer, drive the seal gently onto the end of the valve guide until the seal contacts the top collar. Don't distort the seal.

25. *Install the spring pack, both the inner and outer springs, onto the valve stem. Then cap it off with the top collar, making sure the collar step is inside the top of the springs.*

26. *Compress the springs and install the two keepers into their stem slot. After removing the compressor, tap the end of the spring pack with a plastic hammer to make sure the keepers are set.*

27. *With all valves in their head, figure out what thickness head gasket you need to get the proper squish. (See Chapter 7: Special Procedures for how to do that.) Then put the new gaskets on the heads dry.*

To check the seal-to-collar clearance, measure the inside depth of the valve seals using a dial indicator (ours are 0.370") and measure the outside length (ours are 0.510"). Subtract the inside depth from the outside length. The difference (0.140") is subtracted from the next measurement. Now slip a valve into its guide and install its top collar and keepers. Then measure from the top of the guide to the inside face of the lowest section of the collar (ours is 0.930"). Then subtract the seal measurement you got in the previous step (0.140") to get the seal-to-collar clearance (0.790"). This number must be more than the cam's valve lift spec (0.560"), plus a 0.060" safety clearance. (Ours came to 0.620".)

During assembly, do not get any Loctite on the inner portion of the valve seal or top of the valve guide.

With safety glasses on and the head in a valve spring compressor (with the end of the tool that moves on the top collar), compress the springs and

install the two keepers into the slot made for them in the valve's stem. Then release the compressor so both keepers are held against the inside of the top collar. Finally, tap the end of the spring pack with a plastic hammer to make sure the keepers are set in position and will not pop out later.

There's no need to retorque the head bolts after the engine has been run, no matter which type of head bolt style or head design you're using. However, it's a good idea to check the torque on the cylinder base nuts (if so equipped), lifter blocks, oil pump, rocker covers, and cam cover. However, do not move the hardware if you do not have to. I would set the torque wrench to the lower end of the required torque range and see if the hardware moves. The goal is to see if it loosened up, but not move the hardware if it's not necessary.

Once the heads are on, you can check the timing of the cam using a method outlined in Chapter 7: Special Procedures under the heading Degreeing A Cam if you choose.

  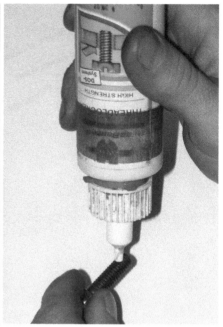

28. To install the heads on a cylinder-stud engine, torque the bolts as per the head manufacturer's specs. Reg likes to let the engine sit for about an hour to stabilize the metal. He then rechecks the final torque.

29. If you're installing the heads as per the H-D sequence, the final turn of the head bolts is the last 1/4-turn. Put a mark on the bolt head and head to ensure you do this right.

30. The final step, if needed, is to install the studs for the exhaust headers. Reg starts by putting a little red Loctite on the head-side of the stud's threads, which is the coarser of the stud's two threads.

CAMSHAFT SPECIFICATIONS

Here are the specs for Andrews' popular EV59 camshaft. Andrews has it listed in its catalog as a modified version of its EV57 camshaft for H-D Evolution engines. The EV59 is designed for a modified 80 to 88-cubic-inch engine with hydraulic lifters that's fitted with performance valve springs and collars. Though the specs are not the same as the R&R proprietary grind camshaft they're installing and computing the valve spring clearances and such for in the accompanying assembly sequence photos, it will give you something you can refer to as he goes through the steps. Numbers with a period and inch mark are distance measurements of valve travel from its valve seat in the head. Plain numbers are degrees of flywheel rotation computed from TDC at the start of the intake stroke. (See Chapter 1: The Bottom End for more info on this.)

EV59 CAM SPECS

Grind Timing (at .053" cam lift): 30/54 intake, 56/24 exhaust.

Duration at .053": 256 intake, 260 exhaust
Duration at .020": 290 intake, 294 exhaust
Valve lift: .560", .560"
Lift at TDC: .236", .208"

HEAD BOLT SEQUENCES

Ensure the head bolts and cylinder studs threads are completely clean of dirt and grime. Then lubricate the head bolt threads, the bottom of the washer (if one is used), and under the head of the bolt where it contacts the head (anywhere you may encounter friction), so you will get a true torque reading. Remember, the head bolts are two different lengths. The long ones go on the pushrod side (right) of the engine, while the short ones go on the primary drive (left) side. The head bolts must be torqued in a specific pattern, to a specific torque setting to prevent head gasket failure and other possible problems. On the front head, the four-bolt order is, when looking at the top of the head with the pushrods to the right: top left (#1), bottom left (#2), top right (#3), and bottom right

(#4). The rear head is the reverse of the front: bottom left (#1), top left (#2), bottom right (#3), and top right (#4).

Starting at bolt #1, torque the bolt to 7-9 ft-lbs. Then do the same for bolt #2, #3, and #4. Then return to bolt #1 and torque it to 12-14 ft-lbs., followed in sequential order by the other three bolts. Now mark each bolt with a line that goes from the bolt head to the cylinder head. Starting again with bolt #1, turn the head bolt 90 degrees (one-quarter turn). (Photo #29 shows a head bolt in its final position.) Then do the other three bolts in sequential order. By the way, not all gasket and head companies require this last step. Be sure to check with the manufacturer of your heads and head gasket to find out what they want.

Some aftermarket head manufacturers use a slightly different torquing procedure than H-D. For example, they may require that you start at bolt #1 and torque it to 7-9 ft-lbs. Then do the same for bolt #2, #3, and #4. Then return to bolt #1 and torque it to 12-14 ft-lbs., followed in sequential order by the other three bolts. You then do this again to a torque of 23, then 35, and a final of 42. They go to a final higher torque, rather than the last 90-degree turn that H-D requires.

Reggie Jr. uses the same sequence and procedure as Harley for the head bolts on all his base stud-style engines, but with a different set of torque values. His head bolts are torqued, in a cross pattern, to 10 ft-lbs., and then progressing in 10 ft-lb. intervals (20, 30, 40, 50) to a final torque of 65 ft-lbs. However, he does not do the last 90-degree turn that H-D requires.

31. *After he threads the stud into the head using his fingers, he threads two nuts onto the exhaust pipe-side of the stud. Then, using two 1/2" wrenches, Reg locks the two nuts against each other.*

32. *He now uses one of the 1/2" wrenches on the outer of the two nuts to install the exhaust stud into the head. Reg then breaks the two nuts apart and removes them from the stud. He does all four studs in this manner.*

Chapter Six

The Valvetrain

Where the pushrods push and the rocker arms rock

If you've been building a complete engine, I've got good news for you. You're almost done and the valvetrain is the easiest section to do. But don't let its apparent simplicity fool you. There's a lot going on in this vital part of your V-twin. Let's run through what the parts do and then talk

a little about your high performance options.

It all starts with the camshaft, which is the controller of what the valvetrain does. In fact, the valvetrain exists simply to transmit the movements of the camshaft to the valves in the heads. As the cam rotates, a lifter rolls up the cam lobe,

No matter what you're building or assembling, don't assume you can work by "feel" and ignore the torque wrench.

which makes it rise in its lifter block and, in turn, lift its pushrod up. As the pushrod rises it pushes up the right arm of the rocker arm it controls. As the rocker rocks on its shaft in response to the pushrod, its other (left) arm presses down against the tip of the valve it controls. The force of the camshaft, as it's driven by the pinion gear, overcomes the pressure of the valve springs and opens the valve to allow in a fresh fuel/air charge into the cylinder if it is an intake valve, or lets the burnt gases escape be it an exhaust valve. Once the lifter reaches the apex of the cam lobe, it starts to descend, which allows the valve springs to return the valve to its seat, sealing its opening once again. The valve springs also force the entire valvetrain associated with that valve to follow the curve of the cam lobe as it drops in height. Each camshaft lobe determines when (timing), how high (lift), and how long (duration) the valve it controls stays open and closed.

Just as some high performance cams require stronger valve springs, aftermarket adjustable pushrods are usually also needed to complete the package. If for no other reason than convenience, you should seriously consider replacing the stock nonadjustable pushrods with a set of adjustable ones. Adjustable pushrods can be installed and removed without having to dismantle the rocker boxes, which saves you time, money (gaskets), and a potential oil leak. As for whether you should use aluminum or steel pushrods, there are pros and cons on

both sides. One of the benefits that the aluminum group states is that since aluminum is lighter, it reduces strain on the rest of the valvetrain. The steel advocates argue that aluminum is more likely to flex, especially when used with stronger performance valve springs, which throws

SPECIAL TOOL LIST

Stiff bristle bottle brushes
Parts cleaning tank
Compressed air supply
Clean shop cloths
Grinder with a fine stone wheel
Wire to hold pushrod tube up
Torque wrench in ft-lbs.
Flat feeler gauge
0.060"-thick wire
Blue Loctite
Extreme pressure lubricant
Assembly lube

The stock H-D rocker arm (right) has a machined pad on one arm, which rubs on the valve's stem and pushes the valve open. The other rocker has a roller instead of a pad, which moves across the valve stem with less friction.

103

the valve timing off and reduces power output. In an effort to give the customer the best of both worlds, some manufacturers offer tapered steel pushrods, which they say, gives the builder the rigidity of steel, but at a lighter weight. I'll leave it to the performance books to help you decide which way to go.

As for the other main component of the valvetrain, the rocker arms, as shown in the opening photo, come in two basic versions: the stock Harley-Davidson pad-style rocker and a roller rocker offered by various aftermarket companies. The stock H-D rocker has a machined pad on the arm that actuates the valve it controls. This pad rubs across the valve stem tip and pushes the valve open. This causes a side load on the valve, which pushes it against its guide and accelerates wear in high-lift applications. That said, the stock H-D version is sufficient in stock and mild cam lift applications. However, when you get to the higher lifts (.550" or more) a roller rocker is the best way to go. The roller rocker has a roller on

the end of the arm that actuates the valve, eliminating the side-load and friction problems.

One variation of the roller rocker is the higher (longer) ratio rocker. This rocker increases the amount that the valve comes off its seat in the head (valve lift) without changing the camshaft. Some performance companies offer this type of roller rocker arm. The longer ratio rocker has its arms in a different position than the stock rocker. The only Harley engine that has a stock 1:1 ratio between cam lift and valve lift is the 1936-47 Knucklehead. Knuckleheads have their rockers' arms at the same height in relation to the pivot point, which is why it is said to have a 1:1 ratio. Since the Knuckle's rocker arms have no offset, the cam lift and valve lift are (theoretically) equal. Panheads have a 1.50:1 rocker ratio. The 1966-69 kidney-shaped cam cover Shovelheads can use the same cams as the cone cam cover Shovelheads, since they both have a rocker arm ratio of 1.42:1. Stock Evo and Twin Cam rocker arms also have the same ratio: 1.625:1, which means the rocker opens the valve 1.625 times the amount of the actual cam lift. You can read about valve and cam lift in Chapter 5: The Heads. A high-lift rocker arm increases this ratio to 1.7:1, 1.75:1, or more depending on the manufacturer. Since these rockers move the valve more, just as a higher lift cam would, you must do the same clearance checks that a cam with more lift or duration would require when assembling the heads. You may also need to install performance valve springs.

Another variation of the roller rocker is one that improves pushrod geometry, specifically the extreme angle of the exhaust

Compare this early-style 1984-92 H-D Evo bottom and middle rocker box sections with the ones used in the second assembly sequence. These boxes don't have an umbrella valve, since these engines are crankcase breathers.

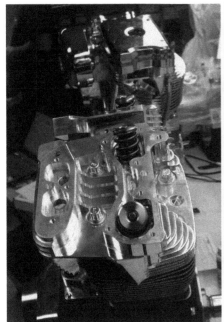  

Assembly sequence #1
1. Opening shot shows the heads installed, torqued down, and ready for the rocker boxes to go on. Reggie will be installing R&R's polished billet units and roller rocker arms, as well as the rest of the valvetrain.

2. With a new gasket on the head, Reggie Jr. bolts on the lower rocker box using the five R&R-supplied bolts and washers and some blue Loctite. A 3/16" Allen is used to just snug the bolts down for now.

3. After putting a little lube on the stem of the supplied umbrella valve, Reggie installs it into its port in the lower box by just pushing it down with his finger until it rests flat against the rocker box.

pushrods, which is a disadvantage shared by all pre-Twin Cam Big Twins. Finally, something that may quiet that annoying exhaust valve tick in the front cylinder!

The valvetrain also takes care of itself, in terms of oil delivery. Pressurized oil from the oil pump is sent to the lifter screen located in the right case (see Chapter 3: The Gearcase) and then to the lifters and their bores in the lifter blocks. Once the lifters pump up, oil travels up the pushrods and into the rocker arms, which lubes the rocker arms and their shafts. Oil spillover from the rocker arms drops onto the valves and spring packs lubricating them and the valve guides. The oily mist that fills the rocker boxes also helps lubricate the moving parts there. Once the oil has done its job in the rocker boxes, it drains back down to the crankcases via oil drain holes in the head and cylinders.

CHANGES

The only major change, actually the only change other than some cosmetic stuff, made to the H-D rocker boxes and the rest of the valvetrain system was the conversion from a crankcase breather system contained in the gearcase section and right crankcase to a head breather system in 1993. On 1984-92 Evo Big Twin engines, the pressurized air/oil mist from the bottom end vents to a fitting in the right crankcase, located just inboard and below the oil pump. A hose connects this fitting to the air cleaner housing, so the air/oil mist from the engine can be sucked into the engine and burned during the combustion event. On 1993-99 Evo models, the scenario is a bit different. Though the pressurized oil system is basically the same, the routing of the pressurized air/oil mist is different. On these engines, this mist travels from the gearcase section, up the pushrod tubes. As the oily air travels up the

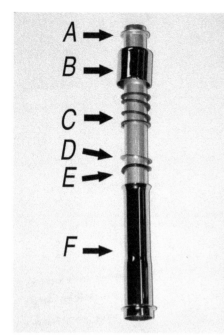

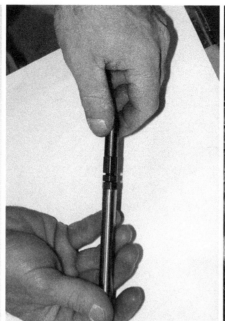

4. Here's how to assemble a pushrod tube: the collar (B), spring (C), flat steel washer (D), and O-ring (E) go onto the upper tube (A), which slides inside the chrome lower tube (F).

5. Check with your pushrod manufacturer regarding how many different length pushrods you have. After Reg marks them so he knows which is which, he shortens all four pushrods as far as they will go.

6. Reg installs the proper new O-rings into both places for the pushrod tubes on both heads and makes sure they are fully seated into their recesses. The lifters for the front cylinder are at their lowest positions.

pushrod tubes, some of the oil separates from the air and returns to the gearcase section via the lifter blocks. As for the now-less oily air, it continues up the pushrod tubes and into the middle section of each rocker box where it passes through a small circular filter element. This filter element's job is to separate the rest of the oil from the air before the air passes through the umbrella valve. Once past the umbrella valve, the now much less oily air passes through the breather port in the right side of the head and enters the air cleaner housing via a hollow bolt in each head. This air is then sucked into the combustion chambers with the fresh outside air and burned during the combustion event.

The stock Harley-Davidson rocker boxes are the only ones that have three sections to them. All the aftermarket versions are two-piece setups. To cover both options, we've included an assembly sequence with photos and captions for each version.

PREP WORK

Start by checking that all passageways in the rocker boxes and rocker arms are clean and clear of debris, be it metal filings or small bits of packing material. Use a stiff bristle bottle brush, a cleaning tank, and some compressed air to clean out all passageways. The ones in the heads should have already been checked and cleaned as described in Chapter 5: The Heads.

Check all threaded holes. Make sure they are free of debris and dirt. Make sure all threads are in good shape and will not strip out when you reinstall whatever goes into them at the correct torque. Now is the time to weld up, machine flat, drill, and rethread a stripped hole.

After spraying a shop cloth with brake clean, wipe off the gasket surfaces of the heads and all rocker box sections to remove any dirt or oily residue. Then check that all gasket surfaces are free of gouges, imprints, marks with depth (if you can feel it with your fingernail, it's too deep), or

 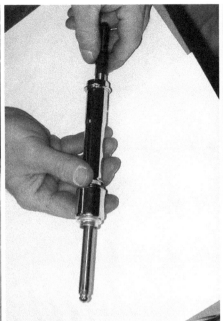 

7. He does the same for both lifter blocks, which get two O-rings per block. With this set of pushrod tubes, each O-ring also gets a steel flat washer under it. Check with your pushrod tube manufacturer.

8. Slip the correct pushrod into an assembled pushrod tube, so the adjustable end is at the bottom of the tube. Do both pushrods and tubes for the cylinder you plan to do first.

9. After lubing both pushrod ends, position the pushrod and its tube in the engine, so the bottom end of each pushrod is on the top of its lifter and the top of the pushrod is protruding into the head.

any other imperfections that may allow oil to get past the gaskets.

Check the condition of all the parts you plan on installing in this section of the build. If you're going to reuse old parts, mark what location they are in as you disassemble the engine, so you can put them back in the same spot (front intake, etc.). This holds true for all valvetrain components. Check all clearances as per the engine manufacturer's spec. This holds true for new as well as used components. How to do this is covered in the section on blueprinting, which is in Chapter 7: Special Procedures.

Look for signs of scuffing or pitting on all components. Check all four rocker arm shafts and the bores of all rocker arms for gouges, scouring marks with depth, or any other imperfections that may cause a problem. Also check the balls on both ends of all the pushrods, as well as the pushrod sockets on the rocker arms. Any grooves

or scoring on the rocker arm bushings or shafts is cause for concern. If you can feel the mark with your fingernail, it's too deep to reuse. Replace the defective part.

If you're reinstalling the used stock non-adjustable pushrods, ensure they're not bent by laying them side-by-side and rolling them on a perfectly flat surface. If no gaps appear between the pushrods as they rotate, they're good to go. Check that the pads of stock rocker arms don't have flat spots on them. If so, use a fine grinding wheel to return them to their proper shape. If you're using roller rockers, check the roller to make sure it's secure and tight to the rocker arm. If they're past the manufacturer's specs, replace them. If a rocker's roller comes apart it will damage components in the head and rocker assembly, and possibly the rest of the engine as well.

Harley-Davidson calls for the following allowable specs and service wear limits for the

10. To build the rocker arm assembly, Reg slips two rocker shafts into the right side of the R&R billet rocker perch. He makes sure the notch in each shaft aligns with the bolthole next to it.

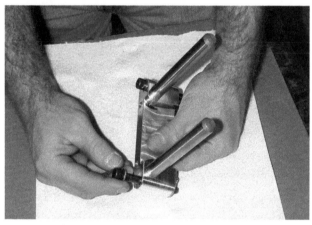

11. Reg then installs both supplied bolts, with their washers, into the perch. The bolts engage the notches in the shafts and hold them in the perch. He then puts a thin coat of assembly lube on both shafts.

12. With assembly lube inside the rocker arms, Reg slips them onto their shafts. Since the perch is on the right side of the engine, the arms of the rocker with the pushrod sockets must go against the perch.

rocker assemblies, as per the service manual for 1993 and 1994 FX/Softail Models (#99482-94). The allowable specs and service wear limits for your year and model engine may be different. Be sure to check the service manual for your engine. The rocker arm shaft's fit in the rocker box should be 0.0007" - 0.0022". If it exceeds 0.0035", the lower box or shaft, whichever is at fault, should be replaced. As for the rocker arm, the shaft's fit in the rocker arm bushing should be 0.0005" - 0.002". If it exceeds 0.0035", the rocker bushing should be replaced. The bushing's fit in the rocker arm should be 0.004" - 0.002". The rocker arm endplay in the lower box should be 0.003" - 0.013". If it exceeds 0.0025", shim the rocker arm as needed.

Check that the oil passages on the rocker boxes line up with the ones on their heads. Do this by laying the new gaskets against the parts in question and then the heads. Do the same for the lifter blocks and right crankcase. If the holes in the part/crankcase line up with the holes in the gasket, you're all set. If not, find out why and correct the problem. Hopefully, you just have the wrong gasket. If you have a head breather, make sure all the breather passageways are clear and aligned.

ASSEMBLY TIPS

As stated at the beginning of this chapter, this is the easiest section to install. However, there are a few things to watch out for. When installing the rocker arm assembly into a custom lower rocker box, the dowels may be a tight fit in the box. If so, gently tap the billet perches down with the base of your hand to get the rocker assembly to rest against the lower box.

When slipping the rocker arm shafts into their rocker arms, make sure the notch in the shaft, which has to align with the bolt hole on the right side of the lower box, will do so once it's fully inside the rocker arm.

When torquing the lower rocker box hardware to spec, do the support bolts first, since they go to a higher torque spec than the five other lower box bolts. Then torque the rest of the bolts in descending-size order.

The stock H-D rocker boxes are not front or rear head specific; neither are most aftermarket versions. That's why you'll find two umbrella valve ports in an aftermarket lower box and in the middle section of the H-D three-piece version. Make sure you install the valve into the port that's just upstream of its breather port in the right face of the head. If you put the valve into the unused port, you're going to get an oily mess all over the right side of your new engine soon after you start riding the bike.

If there's a process that can be screwed up in this section with disastrous results, it's adjusting the pushrods. However, this is not because it's hard to do. You just have to pay attention and give the lifters time to bleed down before rotating the engine to do the pushrods on the other cylinder. To start, remove the spark plugs and rotate the engine so the two lifters for the cylinder you plan on working on are at their lowest point, which is when both lifters are on the heel, or opposite side of the cam lobe. The lifters are on the heel of their cam lobe when the piston for that cylinder is at its TDC point during its compression stroke. Then extend the pushrod until it just contacts both the rocker arm above and the lifter below it. You've got it right if the pushrod spins with a slight drag when you rotate it with your fingers. This is the zero lash point. Then use a black marker to make a reference mark on the side of the pushrod facing you, if the manufacturer has not already put a mark on the pushrod for you. You can now use the necessary wrenches to turn the pushrod out (making it longer) the required amount of turns called for by the pushrod manufacturer. How many turns depends on the pitch of the threads the manufacturer used on the adjuster. Check the instructions that came with your pushrods to see how many turns they want since not all brands are the same.

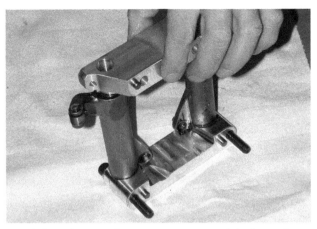

13. The other perch can now go on, with the rocker arm cutouts on the inside and the dowels facing down as on the other perch support.

14. Once Reg slips in the last two bolts with their washers the rocker arm assembly is ready to be bolted into the lower rocker box. Do both rocker arm assemblies at this time and in the same way.

15. Reg prefers to put just a drop of Manley extreme pressure lubricant onto the end of each valve stem for start-up lubrication. He then puts blue Loctite on all four rocker arm bolt threads.

16. Reg installs the rocker assembly into the lower box and torques the four bolts to 20-21 ft-lbs. in a cross pattern using a 1/4" Allen. These bolts get torqued to spec first, since they get a higher torque than the five lower box bolts.

17. Reg can now install and torque the five lower rocker box bolts to 13 ft-lbs. using a 3/16" Allen. They go in all four corners and the center. Don't forget that center one!

18. After putting a wire onto the pushrod tube to hold it out of the way, Reg extends the pushrod as far as he can using just his fingers. He then threads down the locknut.

Once the pushrod is turned out the specified amount of turns, secure the locknut so the adjustment will not change when the engine is running. Some mechanics like to put some blue Loctite theadlocker compound on the adjuster's threads that the locknut will be over. Do the same for the other pushrod for that cylinder. Then wait about 10-20 minutes, so the two hydraulic lifters you just adjusted can bleed down before rotating the engine to get the other cylinder's lifters at their lowest point. If you rotate the engine before the lifters bleed down, the just-adjusted lifters will hold their valves open when they should be closed and they may be bent by the moving piston. And yes, you can bend a valve even if you're moving the engine by hand. You can safely rotate the engine again when you can spin the pushrods you just adjusted with just your fingers. Once you've adjusted the other

cylinder's pushrods, wait another 10-20 minutes, so those hydraulic lifters can also bleed down before you rotate the engine to ensure everything moves easily. You can then pop in the top clips and close up all four pushrod tubes. You can also reinstall the spark plugs.

If you're reinstalling the stock non-adjustable pushrods, there are four different lengths and their locations are determined by their color code. The front intake pushrod is yellow and the rear intake is blue, while the front exhaust is green and the rear exhaust is purple. Make sure you do not swap ends on the stock pushrods. The ball end that was contacting the lifter must do so again, etc. Using the stock non-adjustable pushrods also affects how you torque down the lower rocker box, which must be installed after you've positioned the pushrods on top of their respective lifters, complete with pushrod tubes

19. Using the needed wrenches, Reg adjusts the pushrods as per the manufacturer's specs. Each manufacturer has its own required number of turns for its adjustable pushrods for hydraulic lifters due to thread pitch.

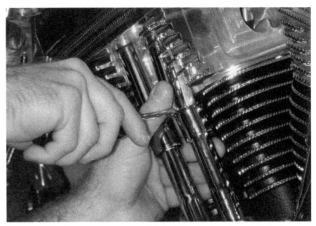

20. Once the adjustments are made and the lifters have bleed down, Reg pops in the top clips for the pushrod tubes using a flat-bladed screwdriver. There's also a special tool you can get to do this.

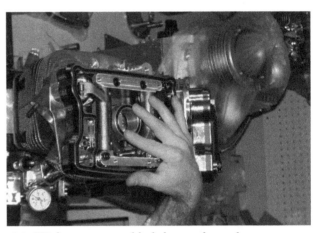

21. With more assembly lube on the rocker arm rollers, Reg installs the square rubber gasket and center O-ring into their grooves in the lower rocker box. He then rotates the engine a few times to make sure everything works as it should.

22. The rocker box cover can now go on using the R&R-supplied bolts, with their gasketed washers. Reg puts some blue Loctite on the bolt threads and torque the bolts to 13 ft-lbs. using a 3/16" Allen in a cross pattern.

and all O-rings. First rotate the engine so the lifters for that cylinder are at their lowest point, just as you would do to install adjustable pushrods. As you torque the lower rocker box hardware down in small increments, follow a crisscross pattern doing one fastener at a time until you reach the final torque values of 15-18 ft-lbs. for the larger bolts and 10-13 ft-lbs. for the smaller ones. The lifters will bleed down after you finish torquing the lower rocker box hardware, so don't rotate the engine for at least 10-20 minutes. You'll know the lifters are bled down when you can spin the pushrods with your fingers. Then do the same for the other rocker arm assembly.

Assembly sequence #2

1. Our opening shot shows a stock H-D head on a workbench with the valve packs installed and ready for the rocker boxes to go on. We'll be installing stock H-D boxes and rocker arms.

2. With a new gasket on the head, secure lower rocker box using the four stock bolts and washers, a 1/2" socket, and blue Loctite. Just snug the bolts down now, so you can check valve springs and collars clearance.

3. With some Manley extreme pressure lubricant on the tip of each valve stem, remove the two bolts on the pushrod side of the rocker box. Then slip the stock H-D rocker arms into the lower box perch.

Aftermarket pushrods may also be four different lengths, though they are usually three with both intakes being the shortest, while the longest is the front exhaust. The rear exhaust pushrod is the middle length one. However, check the manufacturer's instructions to be sure.

When installing the rocker box covers, be they the stock ones or a set of custom rocker boxes, and/or performance valve springs and collars, you must check for sufficient clearance between the valve springs and collars where they get close to the rocker box's inner surfaces. You need at least 0.060" of clearance all around the springs and collars. The easiest way to check is to run a 0.060"-thick wire around the outside of the spring packs as a Go/No Go gauge. Sometimes you can get the clearance you need by just repositioning the rocker box on the head. If not, the rocker box must be removed and machined to get the space the valve springs and collars need. Don't forget to also check that the top collars do not hit the rocker box cover's inner face once it's on. Do

4. After installing two of the lower box bolts (with blue Loctite) into the lower rocker box and putting assembly lube on the rocker shafts, slip the shafts into their rocker arms with the notch aligned with the bolt hole.

this by putting a small lump of clay on the highest point of the collar. Then bolt on the top cover. Now remove the cover and measure the thickness of the clay if it was flattened by the cover. You need a minimum of 0.060" between the bottom of the indentation and the inner face of the rocker box cover.

If, once you're all done and the bike is fired up and running sweet, you find that there's a persistent valve tick coming from the front exhaust pushrod, don't get out the wrenches. There's no way you're going to adjust out the dreaded Evo tick, which is due to the extreme angle that the front exhaust pushrod must work at to reach the rocker arm it controls. (However, you may try the improved geometry rocker arms mentioned earlier.) Now that I've warned you, if you want to waste endless hours trying to adjust it out, go right ahead. I'll be out riding.

6. *Place the middle section onto the lower box. With assembly lube on the stem of a new umbrella valve, install it into the middle section by pushing it down into its port with your finger until it rests flat against the box.*

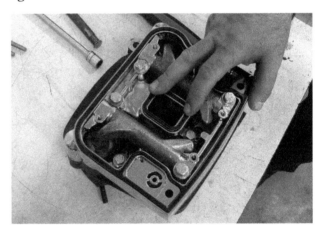

7. *A new rubber gasket is installed into the center groove, as well as in the one around the middle section's perimeter.*

5. *With a new gasket on the lower box, install the lower box hardware with blue Loctite. The support bolts are torqued to 18 ft-lbs. first, the 7/16" socket bolts get 13 ft-lbs. next, and the 1/4" Allen bolts then go to 10 ft-lbs.*

8. *With blue Loctite on all four bolts, install the top rocker box using a 1/4" Allen and torque the bolts to 10 ft-lbs. in a cross pattern. If using performance valve springs and/or collars, check their clearance.*

Chapter Seven

Special Procedures

Building a special engine?
Then you need to do some special procedures

The procedures covered here are presented in the order they're mentioned in the previous six chapters, which means the first ones cover steps that must be done when assembling the bottom end (Chapter 1), and so on. Also included here are some procedures you will only need to do if you are building a specific style of engine, such as a big-bore or stroker motor.

Other procedures, such as Setting The Squish, Measuring The Combustion Chamber, Milling The Heads, and Claying The Pistons are presented in the order they should be done. You should find out what thickness head gasket you'll need to get the squish you want, followed by checking that the combustion chambers are equal in size. If the chambers are mismatched by

2cc or more, the head with the larger chamber will need to be milled. If you're planning on milling the heads and/or cylinders to increase the compression ratio, the head gasket thickness and how much you mill off the head to match the combustion chambers are all part of the computations. Once you have all that squared away, if you're going to run a performance camshaft and/or have the heads reworked, you must clay the tops of the pistons to make sure there's enough clearance between the pistons and valves.

At the end of this chapter are a few other bits of useful information, such as the proper initial heat and cooling cycles you should follow when first starting the engine and the safest way to break-in your new engine.

The procedures you find in this collection are presented in the order they appear in the book. When you're all done, take a look at the very last and possibly most important procedure - the best and safest way to break in that brand new engine.

1: Big Bore Cylinders

Once an owner decides he wants to increase the displacement of his engine, the next question is how to do it? Do you go with bigger bore cylinders or a longer stroke? Each of these methods has advantages and disadvantages, as it is with all things. Both ways give you more horsepower and torque, but not in the same ratios. For the same cubic inch increase, a bigger bore gives more horsepower at high rpm than a stroked motor, but a longer stroke gives more torque down low. Simply put, if only more horsepower is your goal, go bigger bore. A big-bore engine will also last longer than a stroked one, even though the big-bore engine is spinning at a higher rpm more often. This is due to the speed the pistons must move in the cylinders on a long-stroke engine, as well as connecting rod side-loads, but we'll get into that in the section on stroking, which follows this one. A drawback of very large bore engines is that the flame front created by the spark plug has a longer way to travel.

When you have your crankcase cylinder spigots bored out to accommodate the new cylinders, machine the threaded crankcase stud that lives between the cylinders at the same time, so it matches the curve of the new spigot holes. However, once this is done, the stud can only be installed the same way it was machined, so make sure you install it correctly and torque it to spec before machining it. This case and stud were not done correctly.

115

This can affect how much of the air/fuel mixture actually gets burned, as well as increase the chance of detonation.

The best way to get the cubic inch increase you want is to do a bit of both. This way, you get the benefits of both methods and minimize the negative aspects since you're not going with a very large bore or very long stroke. Besides, there's a limit to how big you can go with the cylinders, since you can only bore the spigot holes so far before you run out of crankcase. That's another reason why builders who want very large displacement engines must also increase the engine's stroke. Of course, if big bore is what you want, you can buy a set of crankcases with much larger cylinder spigots from S&S, STD, or other manufacturers.

Since we're on the subject of crankcase, the 1984-86 factory crankcases are very good, but after that the quality varied. Carefully check 1987-88 crankcases to make sure you have one of the good sets. The 1989-93 cases can be really bad. They were made from poor-quality aluminum alloy with equally poor castings. These year cases are plagued with multiple problems, including cracks, casting porosity that allows oil from the lower end to seep out of the engine, loose sprocket shaft inserts, and cylinder studs that pull out of the cylinder decks. Owners of these year crankcases should read Chapter I: The Bottom End, where I explain this

Once an owner decides he wants to increase the displacement of their engine, the next question is how to do it?

A drawback of very large bore engines is that the flame front created by the spark plug has a longer distance to travel.

issue, as well as your options, in detail.

To install a set of bigger bore cylinders onto your Evo-style engine, you'll need to have the cylinder spigots bored out to the size recommended by the cylinder maker. This is not something to do in the home garage. Get the specs from the manufacturer and bring the cylinders and crankcases to a qualified machine shop. The cases have to be bolted together just as they will be when they are part of a running engine. The hardware must also be torqued to spec. You'll also want to have the threaded crankcase stud that lives between the cylinders machined to match the curve of the new spigot holes, so the cylinder spigots will clear it.

After the crankcases are machined, there's no real difference between installing big-bore cylinders compared to stock ones. Be sure to check with the cylinder and piston manufacturers to get their recommendations on piston-to-cylinder clearances, as well as any special requirements after initial start-up. Chapter 4: The Cylinders gives you an assembly sequence for both types of cylinder mounting styles. Just follow these, as well as the cylinder and piston manufacturer instructions, and you'll be good to go.

2: Building A Stroker

The big question, once you've decided to go for more cubic inches, is how to do it. Besides trying to weld on another cylinder, which I don't recommend, the only two options are bigger bore cylinders or a longer stroke. Each of these methods has advantages and disadvantages – as discussed in the Big Bore section a couple of pages back. Both ways give you more horsepower and torque, but not in the same ratios.

As I mentioned in that section, the smart choice is to do a bit of both to achieve the engine size you want. This way, you get the all the benefits with minimum drawbacks since you're not going with a very large bore or very long stroke. As for the actual work involved, the only difference between building a long stroke engine and building a stock stroke one is that you have to ensure there is enough clearance for the connecting

rods and pistons to travel the extra distance.

Before we go any further with the idea of adding to the stroke of your engine, you should check your crankcases, which is covered in the Big Bore section.

Moving the location of the crankpin, and, therefore, the bottom of the connecting rods, but not the top, changes the angle at which the rods work and widens the arc in which they move. It also increases the mechanical advantage (leverage) of the connecting rods on the flywheel assembly. This results in an increase in torque across the engine's entire rpm range, but mostly at low rpm.

1. Best way to check the clearances on a stroker is to pull the complete flywheel assembly into the left case and install the pistons (no rings) and cylinders so you can check clearances for all 360 degrees of rotation.

2. Some case material may need to be removed to get a minimum of 0.060" of clearance between the rods and cases at all points of flywheel assembly travel. The section between the two cylinder spigots is a common trouble area.

117

The biggest drawback to stroking a motor is accelerated wear due to excessive piston speed and connecting rod side-load. On a stock stroke Evo engine, the piston moves 4-1/4" up and down the cylinder with every full rotation of the flywheel assembly. At idle, it does this 1,000 times per minute, which is written as 1000 revolutions per minute, or rpm. When you increase the distance the piston has to travel, which is what you're doing by making the stroke longer, the piston still has to travel the entire length of the cylinder in the same amount of time: one minute. To do that, it must move faster. Small increases in piston speed don't really adversely affect engine life, but large ones do.

4. The interfaces between the rods and flywheels must also be checked, especially if I-beam connecting rods are being used. One possible trouble spot is this section of flywheel.

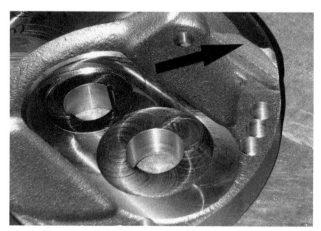

5. This area of the flywheels (arrow) had to be machined to get the needed clearance for the connecting rods selected.

How long is too long depends on what you plan on doing with the engine. However, most builders would agree that a 4-1/2" stroke, which is a 1/4" increase, is relatively safe, with 4-5/8" not being a big issue either. That 1/4" increase in stroke is achieved by moving the crankpin 1/8" farther from the axis of the flywheel assembly. This pushes the piston 1/8" higher in the cylinder and pulls it 1/8" lower in the cylinder. As you would expect, changes have to be made so the piston doesn't slam into the head at its TDC point or into the flywheel assembly at BDC. (If you're unfamiliar with these terms, read Chapter 1: The Bottom End.) The additional angle of the connecting rods, while giving them more leverage, also increases their side load pressure. This means the pistons are pushed harder against one side of their cylinder's bore. Again, a moderate increase in stroke gives you the gains and minimizes the accelerated wear factor.

Since the connection rods are going to follow a wider arc and the pistons will travel farther in their

3. Since the crankpin nuts will also follow a wider arc inside the cases, they may contact ridges on the inner walls. S&S sells an excellent little gauge that makes it easy to see where material has to be removed to get the 0.060" minimum.

cylinder bores, the clearances for these components must be checked for the full 360 degrees of flywheel rotation. The areas affected by a longer stroke are the crankcases, flywheels, connecting rods, cylinders, and pistons. The best way to check the clearances on all these components is to pull the complete flywheel assembly into the left case using an old set of Timken bearings. Then slip the pistons onto their respective connecting rods, without wrist pin clips or piston rings. The cylinders can now go over their pistons, with base gaskets on the cases. Don't torque them; just snug the cylinders down.

As the connecting rods follow the crankpin, they swing to the front and rear of the crankcase spigot holes. Due to the wider arc of their swing, the clearance they have at the points where they come near the cases must be checked. If needed, material is removed to get a minimum of 0.060" between the rods and crankcases at all points of the flywheel assembly's 360 degrees of rotation.

The same must be done for the crankpin nuts, which are now also following a wider arc inside the crankcases. The possible contact areas for the nuts are the inner walls of the cases. S&S sells an excellent little gauge that makes it easy to know where you have to remove material for the crankpin nuts. Only remove the minimum amount needed. Small amounts will not affect the integrity of the cases, but excessive amounts, especially in the wrong areas, will.

The next areas affected by the wider arc of the rods are the flywheels and rods themselves. However, modern stroker flywheel manufacturers usually make their flywheels with plenty of clearance for their intended stroke. Ditto for performance connecting rods. However, they may not have checked with the style of connecting rod you're going to use. And rod-to-rod clearance may be a concern when using Harley-Davidson rods, since they're manufactured with the stock stroke in mind. The smart mechanic checks to be sure.

The cylinders are the next components that

6. Though not usually a problem on performance connecting rods, rod-to-rod clearance in this section may be a concern when using Harley-Davidson rods.

7. Check the cylinders for proper clearance for the connecting rods. The affected area is the notch that's already cut into the cylinder spigot for the rods. A Dremel tool can be used to get the standard 0.060" minimum.

119

8. *On stroker pistons, the piston skirt that the connecting rod swings near when moving through its arc will have a notch cut into it to give the rod the room it needs. Check it to be sure it's sufficient.*

must be checked for proper clearance for the connecting rods. The affected area is the notch that's already cut into the cylinder spigot for the rods. The wider arc the rods are now following may bring them too close to, or even hit, the cylinder spigot. The standard 0.060" minimum holds true here, too. A hand grinding tool, like a Dremel, will usually do the trick. Be sure to radius any grinding reliefs to ensure no cracks will form in any sharp edge. Don't forget to also remove all tooling marks and burrs.

Last on the list are stroker pistons, which are designed for a specific bore, stroke, and dome shape. One of the piston skirts, the one that the connecting rod swings near when moving through its arc, will have a notch cut into it to give the connecting rod the room it needs to pull the piston down farther in its cylinder. This notch also keeps the rear skirt of the front piston from kissing the front skirt of the rear piston, since they now come down farther. To keep the piston from slamming into the head as it travels farther up the cylinder, a stroker piston is not as tall as stock one. In fact, on a very long stroke motor the piston may be so short that the oil ring groove actually cuts across the wrist pin holes. To keep it from hitting the flywheels when at BDC, a stroker piston usually has shorter skirts than a stocker.

9. *To keep it from slamming into the head, a stroker piston is not as tall as stock one. To keep it from hitting the flywheels when at BDC, a stroker piston usually has shorter skirts.*

3: Balancing

A Harley-Davidson V-twin engine, like all reciprocating piston engines, has an assembly that converts the up and down motion of the pistons into a rotating force. In our V-twins that task is handled by the flywheel assembly that's housed in the crankcases. This flywheel assembly has both rotating and reciprocating components. The rotating components are the parts that only rotate, such as the two flywheels, the pinion shaft, the sprocket shaft, the crankpin, the crankpin bearings and their cages, and the connecting rods. The reciprocating parts are the ones that move up and down and they include the pistons, piston rings, wrist pins, wrist pin clips (or buttons), and connecting rods. Yes, the connecting rods are both rotating and reciprocating components. Since the bottom, or crank pin (CP), ends of the rods are connected to the flywheels at the crankpin, these ends rotate with the flywheels and must be figured in with the rotating parts. The top, or wrist pin (WP), ends of the connecting rods are the ends that are attached to the pistons via the wrist pins. Since they move up and down with the pistons, they are part of the reciprocating component list.

A quick look at a flywheel assembly shows you that some of the rotating components and all of the reciprocating ones are attached to the flywheels at a point away from the center of the wheels. This, of course, throws the flywheels out of balance. To bring the flywheels somewhat back into balance and significantly reduce the engine's vibration, each flywheel is made with a counterweight cast into it. This counterweight is positioned directly opposite the crankpin's location, so it can best offset the weight of the rotating and reciprocating components attached there. These counterweights are made to a standard size. To get the flywheel assembly as balanced as possible, the mechanic weighs all the parts to be used and, with the help of a mathematical formula, figures out whether he needs to remove or add weight to the flywheel counterweights. If he has to remove weight, he drills holes into the counterweights at specific locations. To add weight, which is not usually the case, he drills holes in the counterweights and then fills them with a metal (usually a heavy tungsten alloy) that weighs more than the steel he

The first step in balancing a flywheel assembly is to make sure the beam balance is calibrated and accurate. With all weights on zero, the end of the balance beam should be hovering right in the middle of its slot, at the zero mark, in the far end of the weight scale. Then put a known weight on the plate, move the balance's weights to the proper spots, and see if the balance gives you a correct reading.

SPECIAL TOOL LIST

Beam balance and test weight
Bobweight assembly
Balance stand and shafts
Electric drill and bits
Dremel grinder
Carpenter's level
0.060"-thick wire

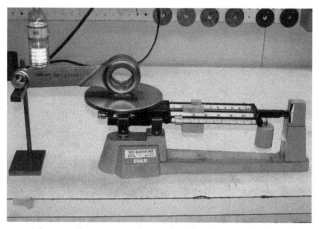

1. After making sure the rod is level, put the small end of the rod on a balance support and the large end on the balance. Once you get the rod's rotating weight, record the CP number on the balance worksheet. Do both rods.

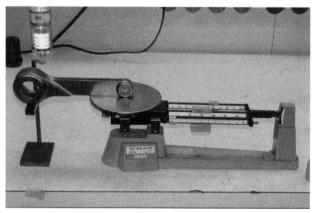

2. After making sure the rod is level, put the large end of the rod on a balance support and the small end on the balance. Once you get the rod's reciprocating weight, record the WP number on the balance worksheet. Do both rods.

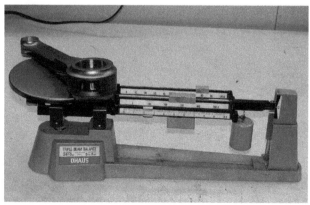

3. Now put the entire rod on the balance's platform and record its total weight on the balance worksheet. Then do the same for the other rod.

drilled out. Sometimes he drills the edge of the wheels near the crankpin.

Once you have sized, selected, machined, and have on hand all the actual parts that are going to be assembled into and onto the flywheel assembly, which includes the pistons and their various components, you're ready to static balance the engine. That means the crankpin bearings should be fitted to the connecting rods, the pistons and their rings are fitted to their cylinders, the wrist pin bushings in the connecting rods are reamed, etc. To properly balance the engine all the needed components must be at the actual weight they will be when installed into the engine. You cannot accurately do this phase of the build using a proxy part, as you can when, for example, you're checking for the correct size Timken spacer for the main bearing assembly on the sprocket shaft. Taking any shortcuts during the balancing procedure will introduce unwanted error into your computations. To walk you through the static balancing process step-by-step we documented how one of R&R Cycle's techs balanced one of R&R's 131" engines. Just substitute your numbers for the ones he got.

The first step in static balancing a flywheel assembly is to make sure the balance beam is calibrated and accurate. With all weights on zero, the end of the balance beam should be hovering right in the middle of its slot, at the zero mark, in the far end of the weight scale. There is an adjusting screw at the plate end of the balance that you use to zero

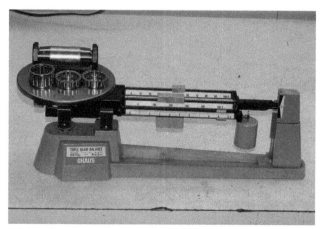

4. With the hard part out of the way, weight the crankpin assembly, which includes the woodruff key, both crankpin nuts, all roller bearings, all three bearing cages, and the crankpin. Record their weight on the worksheet.

the balance, if needed. Then put a known weight on the balance's platform, move the balance's weights to the proper spots, and see if the balance beam gives you a correct reading.

As for the calculations, here's how you arrange and add up the numbers you get. We'll use the weights our R&R tech got. But first, a little bit of controversy: some builders insist that both piston assemblies must be the same total weight. Others feel this is not necessary since the total weight of the two pistons combined is what pushes on the crankpin, which is why the total weight of both is used in the balance equation. Personally, I'd go with making them the same weight. I don't know if it makes a difference, but it sure can't hurt. If needed, remove material from the underside of the dome and/or around the connecting rod slot in the piston skirt of the heavier piston with a Dremel grinding tool. If you work on the piston skirt, make sure you smooth it back out when you're done.

At right are the specs R&R got (in grams) when they weighed this 131" engine's components.

Though most of this is self evident, there are a few terms that we should go over like the values Total and Actual as listed in the front and rear connecting rod columns. The Total figure is what you get when you add up the crankpin end weight (CP End) and the wrist pin end weight (WP End). The Actual value is what each connecting rod weighed when the entire rod was measured, not just the WP or CP end. If there's a difference between the Total and Actual numbers it must not be more than 1 gram. As you can see, the CP End and WP End values are used in the computations. The Actual value is taken to check that the other two partial values are correct.

The next thing to cover is the balance factor, which is the percentage of the total reciprocating weight that will be used in the computations. R&R uses 60 percent, which is the standard for a street motor. Drag racing motors, which are run at high-rpm, usually get 55-58 percent. As I understand it,

Harley uses 52 percent, while S&S likes 60. When static balancing, no balance factor is going to make a 45-degree V-twin run smoothly at all rpm speeds. Different balance factors just move the vibration up or down the engine's rpm range.

The formula that's used to determine the weight of the bobweight needed for the balancing and drilling part of this procedure is: (Reciprocating Weight x Balance Factor) + (Rotating Weight)/2. Once you have the adjusted reciprocating weight,

---

PISTON ASSEMBLIES

Front Piston	Rear Piston
Piston: 569.5	Piston: 569.5
Wrist pin: 128.0	Wrist pin: 128.5
Clips: 37	Clips: 37
Rings: 52	Rings: 51.5
Total: 786.5	Total: 786.5

Total For Both Pistons: 1,573

CONNECTING ROD ASSEMBLIES

Crankpin	Front Rod	Rear Rod
Pin: 522	WP End: 250	WP End: 247
Nuts: 93	CP End: 363	CP End: 635
Cages:	Total: 613	Total: 882
Bearings: 83	Actual: 612	Actual: 882
Key: 1		
Total: 760		

THE CALCULATIONS

Reciprocating Weight	Rotating Weight
Total For Both Pistons: 1,573	Total For Crankpin: 760
WP End Of Front Rod: 250	CP End Of Front Rod: 363
WP End Of Rear Rod: 247	CP End Of Rear Rod: 635
Total Reciprocating Wt: 2,070	**Total Rotating Wt: 1,758**

Multiply Total Reciprocating Weight: 2,070
By Balance Factor of 60 Percent: 0.60
Adjusted Reciprocating Weight: 1,242

Add Total Rotating Weight: 1,758
Total Bobweight For Both Flywheels: 3,000
Divide Bobweight Total by: 2
Total Bobweight for Each Flywheel: 1,500 grams

which is the result of the reciprocating weight times the balance factor, all there's left to do is add this answer to the total rotating weight. This gives you the total amount of weight that all these components exert on the two flywheels. Since each flywheel is balanced separately, the total weight is divided by 2, which gives you what the bobweight for each flywheel should be in grams. A bobweight is attached to each flywheel in place of the connecting rods and other components to make this phase of the process easier to do.

After the bobweight is attached to one of the flywheels at the crankpin location, a machined shaft is attached to the flywheel/bobweight assembly where the sprocket or pinion shaft, as the case may be, would go. This entire assembly is then positioned on a leveled stand. When you let go of the bobweighted flywheel, it will rotate on the machined shaft until its heaviest point is at the bottom. This is where a little experience makes things easier. How fast the flywheel settled with its heavy side down gives you a clue as to how much material to remove from the section of flywheel at the very lowest (6 o'clock) point. R&R suggests drilling only one 1/2"-wide hole about 3/8" deep and testing the wheel again. The flywheel's counterweight is usually the heaviest section, so the hole is drilled into the side of it along the inside face of the flywheel's edge. The static balancing process is finished when the flywheel does

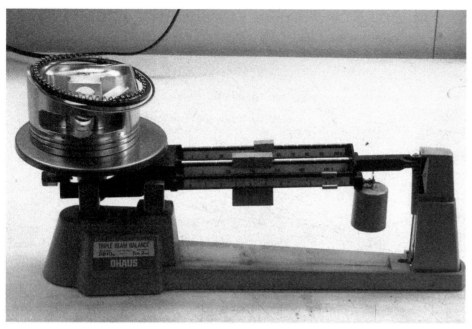

5. Each piston assembly is done as a group, which includes all piston rings, the oil ring expander, the wrist pin, and both wrist pin clips (or buttons, as the case may be). Do each piston separately and record their weight on the worksheet.

6. After doing the math on the worksheet, you'll know what weight to make the bob weight, which is made up of different size and weight washers and plates. Weigh the finished bobweight to make sure you're on the money.

not rotate no matter what position you put it in on the leveled balancing stand. Try it in at least three different positions, then do the same for the other flywheel.

DYNAMIC BALANCING

The static balancing process is called that because the flywheel assembly is not in motion when it's being balanced. Static balancing is done before the flywheels are assembled and it's the way Harley engines have been balanced for decades. However, dynamic balancing is the better way to reduce vibration and frictional horsepower losses. The standard practice for dynamically balancing has the completely assembled and trued flywheel assembly rotated at several hundred rpm. There are only two shops I know of that dynamically balance flywheel assemblies: S&S Cycle and R&R Cycle.

S&S Cycle dynamically balances nearly all of its complete flywheel assemblies. S&S flywheel sets that are not purchased assembled, and some special order flywheel assemblies, are static balanced. S&S will rebalance S&S flywheels, but does not offer this service for stock flywheels at this time. S&S has two dynamic balancing systems, which are custom-built Hoffman machines. Here's how they work: The flywheel assembly is placed on the machine with the rods in a cradle that moves up and down as the flywheel turns. The machine spins the flywheels via a belt on the right flywheel and senses the vibration. The flywheels are then stopped and two drills come in from either side to drill the correct amount of material from the correct spot on the rim of the flywheel. There's a sleeve around the drills and all the chips are removed by suction, so nothing gets into the connecting rod bearings. The flywheel is then spun up again to ensure the balance is correct. You can tell if your S&S flywheels have been dynamic balanced by the drill holes. If

7. Attach the bobweight to a flywheel and put the flywheel on the balancing shaft. You know the flywheel is balanced when you can rotate the flywheel into any position and it will not move to any specific location. Then do the other flywheel.

8. As needed, the flywheel is drilled in specific locations to remove weight and make the wheel balanced. The flywheel on the left is drilled and balanced, while the one on the right is fresh.

125

9. This is one of S&S Cycle's Hoffman dynamic balancing machines. It rotates the flywheel assembly via a belt on the right flywheel. The connecting rods have a single bobweight attached to them.

10. The R&R Cycle Hines computerized balancing system also rotates the flywheel assembly via a belt on the right flywheel but it has a bobweight attached to each connecting rod.

they are dynamically balanced, the drill holes will be on the outside face of the flywheels. If static-balanced, the drill holes will be on the inside face of the flywheels.

R&R Cycle's dynamic balancing system is used on all its complete flywheel assemblies. R&R will also dynamically balance any flywheel assembly it builds for a customer, as well as a flywheel assembly built somewhere else. R&R's dynamically balancer started as a standard Hines machine. The owners of R&R then spent the next 2-1/2 years working with the manufacturer to make the machine operate the way R&R wanted. The R&R computerized system also rotates the flywheel assembly via a belt on the right flywheel and senses the vibration. Mounted onto the connecting rods are bobweights that are the exact weight of the piston assemblies that will soon be attached to the end of the rods. Variables, such as flywheel shaft and connecting rod flex, can cause imbalances that create unnecessary vibration. The computer uses sensors to measure the balance of the flywheels, identifies where the imbalance is, and suggests exactly how much material to remove and where to remove it. The flywheels are then stopped, and the required size and depth holes are drilled exactly where specified by the computer on the machine's screen. The drill shavings are kept from getting into the connecting rod bearings during the process. The flywheels are then spun again to ensure the flywheel assembly is now balanced.

4: Pinion Shaft Runout

This test is easy to do and requires only a dial indicator and a means of supporting it, so you can lay the indicator against the side of the pinion shaft. Once the dial indicator is securely fastened, rotate the engine and note how much the shaft moves the dial indicator's needle. A fluctuation of 0.003" or less is fine. However, 0.004" to 0.005" will cause excessive vibration, while anything over 0.005" is cause for concern. The flywheel assembly should be about 0.001", so a fluctuation that high means the flywheels are way out of true and should be removed and repaired as needed.

If you don't have one, you need to buy a dial indicator and mount to check the runout. It's not all bad, as you'll find it's a very useful tool to have in the toolbox.

Though checking pinion shaft runout is something that gets done while assembling and truing the flywheel assembly, it's included here for builders who are not going to split the crankcases but have the gearcase compartment open to install a camshaft.

SPECIAL TOOL LIST

Dial indicator and support

5: Checking Cam Gear Lash

It's important to get the gear lash between the cam gear and pinion gear correct. Too tight a fit will cause a loud whining sound to come from the gearcase compartment. While this may be annoying, the gear tooth and bearing damage that's also occurring will be a lot more of a problem. A slight whine, however, is normal and not a cause for concern.

Having too much lash results in a clicking sound that may lead you to think your lifters are out of adjustment, but no real damage is occurring. The clicking is actually from the teeth on the cam and pinion gears tapping into each other as each lifter roller passes the highest point on its respective cam lobe. As the roller goes over the lobe's peak the pressure on the cam gear changes direction. This forces the cam gear teeth, which were pressed hard against one pinion gear tooth to now shift and press against the one opposite it. As the cam gear tooth moves from one pinion gear tooth to the other, if the gap between the teeth is more than 0.002", the result is a click that's loud enough for you to hear over all the other noises your engine is making.

1. Start by measuring the cam gear using a set of measuring pins, a rubber band, and the micrometer than can go up to 3". Put the pins exactly opposite each other. Then write down the number you get.

Pinion Gear Size Chart

COLOR	PART #	PINION GEAR SIZE	CAM GEAR SIZE
Orange	24040-93	1.4853"/1.4850"	2.7472"/2.7476"
White	24041-93	1.4849"/1.4846"	2.7477"/2.7481"
Yellow	24042-93	1.4845"/1.4842"	2.7482"/2.7486"
Red	24043-93	1.4841"/1.4838"	2.7487"/2.7491"
Blue	24044-93	1.4837"/1.4834"	2.7492"/2.7496"
Green	24045-93	1.4833"/1.4830"	2.7497"/2.7501"
Black	24046-93	1.4829"/1.4826"	2.7502"/2.7506"

SPECIAL TOOL LIST

3" micrometer
Two measuring pins
  (0.105" or 0.108")
Rubber bands

The simple fix is to do the job right the first time, when you're assembling the engine. You can either use the method Reggie Jr. at R&R Cycle uses, which is real simple, effective, and requires only your fingers, or you can check the lash the standard way, using measuring pins and a 3" micrometer. Reg's method is shown in the assembly sequence of Chapter 3: The Gearcase, while the pin method is what we'll go through now. Also, when assembled at the factory, a dot the color of the pinion gear size is painted on the pinion gear. However, you should check it anyway.

Start by measuring the cam gear using the pins required for your year pinion gear and camshaft. The 1984-89 H-D cam gears, which have a single groove cut into their outer face, are measured using 0.105" diameter pins. The 1990-99 cam gears have two grooves cut into their outer face and require the 0.108" diameter pins. As for the aftermarket cam manufacturers, they may give their measurements using either the 0.105" or 0.108" diameter pins, so be sure to check.

Once you've established which pins to use, place the pins exactly opposite each other in the gap between the cam gear teeth and hold the pins in place with a rubber band. Using a 3" micrometer, measure the distance between the two pins and write the number down. Then do the same for the pinion gear you intend to use. Now compare your gears diameters with the accompanying chart, which is

from a H-D service manual. Most aftermarket camshaft manufacturers make their cams as per the red (middle) size, which is acceptable to most pinion gears found in engines. However, if the pinion gear you have is not the correct match for your new camshaft, buy the correct pinion gear from a quality aftermarket supplier. (Don't buy cheap parts!)

2. Then measure the pinion gear you plan on using in the same way, with the pins exactly opposite each other, and write down the number you get.

6: Degreeing A Camshaft

Ever wonder why identical engines don't make the same power? One reason is the difference in cam timing. Though both cams have the same specs (lift, duration, etc.), the timing is a couple of degrees off on one, while the other is right on the money. This is mostly due to the tolerances between the camshaft and flywheels, and/or the cam's gear not being installed onto the cam's shaft at exactly the right spot. Degreeing (measuring) the cam's actual timing in relation to its spec sheet allows you to correct its timing if needed. This is done by removing the cam's gear using a small hydraulic press and then reinstalling it at the proper location.

The cam in an Evo, like on earlier overhead valve Big Twins, has all four lobes on one shaft. Since you can't alter how the lobes relate to each other, you should time the cam by the most important cam event, front intake valve closing. There are two ways to do this: with the heads on the engine or with them off. We'll describe both methods here, but the photos and captions will show you how to do the job with the heads off.

To check the cam with the heads on, the engine can be fully assembled, except for the front cylinder pushrods and tubes. However, the procedure can also be done with just the pinion gear and camshaft properly installed, as well as the cam cover. The front lifter block and lifters must also be installed. After removing the timing hole plug in the left case, attach a degree wheel to the sprocket shaft and secure an indicator to the crankcases. An easy connection point for the indicator is the top crankcase bolt located between the two cylinders.

Start by rotating the engine in the normal direction of travel until the front piston is at the top of its stroke, or as close as you can get it by looking through the spark plug hole. Then set the indicator to the 0 degree mark on the degree wheel. Then screw a TDC locating pin into the front spark plug hole until it hits the top of the piston, then back it off a couple of turns. Rotate the engine forward until the piston is stopped by the TDC locating pin. Note what the degree wheel is reading. Then rotate the engine in the opposite direction and again note what the degree wheel reads. Split the difference between the two points and that is

SPECIAL TOOL LIST

Degree wheel for H-Ds
Dial indicator and clamp
TDC locator
Small hydraulic press

This engine has the minimum parts needed to check camshaft timing: the front piston (minus rings and clips), the front cylinder (with two nuts holding it onto the cases), the pinion gear and camshaft under the cam cover, and the front lifter block and lifters.

the engine's true TDC point. Reset the degree wheel, so it's 0 is at the engine's TDC point and run the test again to make sure you have it right. For example, if the degree wheel indicated 26 degrees BTDC in one direction and 20 ATDC in the other, split the difference between the two (three degrees) and move the degree wheel accordingly. Then run the test again. If you readjusted the wheel correctly, the degree wheel will stop at 23 degrees ATDC and 23 degrees BTDC. Your wheel is now indicating the engine's true TDC point. You can remove the TDC locating pin and measure when the front intake valve closes.

Mount a dial indicator over the front intake lifter, so it's in line with the movement of the lifter. Rotate the engine in the same direction as when it's running. Do not turn it backwards during this part of the procedure, since lash between the gears will throw your measurements off. Use a dial indicator to tell when the lifter is on the heel, or lowest section of its cam lobe. Then zero the indicator out.

Since we want to check when the front intake valve closes, slowly rotate the engine until it reaches and passes its maximum cam lift point. As the lifter descends watch the indicator. When it reaches 0.053", or 0.020" if that is what your cam spec sheet calls for, stop and read what the pointer is indicating on the degree wheel. Check this against the cam's spec sheet for intake valve closing. Be sure to run this test at least twice to make sure you get the same answer each

time before you remove the cam gear.

If the cam's timing is off, make marks on the cam gear and shaft, so you know where to put the gear to correct the problem. Then use a small hydraulic press to remove and reinstall the gear in the proper spot. Then run the test again to see if the cam's timing has been corrected.

1. With the front piston at TDC, mount a dial indicator on the front cylinder and zero it out. Rotate the engine forward and backward to move the piston a few times to ensure the indicator is set at zero when the piston is at TDC. Then set the degree wheel at zero at TDC.

When building a maximum-effort racing engine, some mechanics will also check the timing for the rear intake valve closing spec. If there is a discrepancy, they remove the cam gear and split the difference between the two, since you can't move the gear to a different spot for the rear and front cylinders.

Before you move to the next phase of the engine build, check the timing marks on the left flywheel. You'll need a small mirror and flashlight to see into the timing hole in the left case. Rotate the engine to the TDC point and see if the flywheel TDC mark is in the timing hole as it should be. Do the same for the ignition timing mark.

To check the cam timing with the heads off, the engine's bottom end should be fully assembled, but the gearcase section only needs to have the pinion gear and camshaft (with only its thrust washer) installed. Make sure the cam's timing mark is properly aligned to the pinion gear. The cam cover should also be on. The pistons are on their connecting rods, with or without rings and such. The cylinders are over the pistons, but they only have nuts holding them snugly onto the crankcases. The front lifter block and lifters are also installed, but the pushrods and tubes are not. With the engine setup in this manner, you can check the cam's timing. After removing the timing hole plug in the left case, attach a degree wheel to the sprocket shaft and secure an indicator to the cases, as described earlier. Using the procedure outlined in the photos and captions, find true TDC and reset the degree wheel accordingly. Then follow the same procedure described earlier to check and adjust the cam's timing. Remember, check the cam's timing at least twice to make sure you get the same result before you remove the cam gear.

2. To tell when the front intake lifter is on the heel, or lowest section of its cam lobe, as well as when the cam will close the intake valve, mount a dial indicator over the lifter, so it's in line with the movement of the lifter.

7: Setting The Squish

Unlike earlier H-D overhead valve engines, which have a hemispherical combustion chamber design, the Evo has a quench, also called a squish, band. That changeover was a major leap forward for H-D.

While it's traveling in the intake tract, you want the air/fuel mixture to flow as smoothly as possible, without any turbulence. When you have laminar flow, which is when all the air and fuel molecules are flowing harmoniously through the intake tract, you get the fastest flow, and therefore, the most air/fuel mixture entering the cylinder. However, once the mixture has entered the cylinder you want it to encounter as much turbulence as possible. Turbulence helps mix the air and fuel, so it's completely blended. A thoroughly mixed and proper air-to-fuel ratio combination burns the most efficiently. That means you get the most power out of what you get into the combustion chamber. After all, if only half of what entered the combustion chamber burns, you only got half the power you should have from that air/fuel charge. The rest was wasted and pushed out of the exhaust pipe. To get the maximum power out of the engine component combination you have, you want to get as much air and fuel into the cylinder as possible, mix it so 100 percent of the air is combined with 100 percent of the fuel, and ignite it at just the right time so you get as much useful work out of the expanding hot gases as possible.

On a D-shaped combustion chamber head, when the flat-topped piston rises on its compression stroke, it's mixing the air and fuel in the cylinder by creating turbulence as it also compresses the mixture. When the piston gets very close to its TDC point, the air and fuel that are caught between the piston and flat (D) section of the head are squeezed out at a very high speed, which does two important things. First, it creates lots of turbulence, which really mixes up the air and fuel. Second, it pushes all the mixture in the cylinder into the area where the spark plug is waiting to ignite it, so the flame front created by the spark plug has easy and fast access to the air and fuel mixture. The result is a faster and more complete burning of the mixture and a much higher power

output than you would ever get with the old hemi-head design found on Shovelheads, Panheads, or Knuckleheads.

Many years ago, way before the advent of the Twin Cam, aftermarket performance head gurus were using bathtub-shaped combustion chamber designs. The advantage of this setup is that it has two squish bands working for it instead of one, which results in more of the benefits you get with the D-shaped chamber.

Now that you understand why having a squish band is important, the question becomes how much squish is best? H-D calls for a 0.025" - 0.040" squish band in its service manuals. However, many engine builders feel anything under 0.030" is too small a gap

```
SPECIAL TOOL LIST
─────────────────────
Dial indicator with flat base
```

1. To check the squish band, install two hold-down nuts onto the cylinder studs to pull the cylinder fully down onto the crankcases. Tighten the nuts until they are good and snug, but don't bring them near the torque spec.

3. Cometic Gasket makes various size gaskets, so you can get the squish you want whether the piston is below the cylinder top deck when at TDC, above it, or level with it.

2. Rotate the engine to bring the piston to TDC and position a dial indicator on the top of the cylinder to make sure you have the piston at true TDC. Then use the same dial indicator to see where the piston is in relation to the top deck of the cylinder.

for a street engine that, hopefully, will not be taken apart for a long time. Carbon buildup on the top of the piston and head surface can close the 0.025" gap and allow the piston to contact the head, causing engine damage. Most agree that a squish of 0.030" - 0.040" is the way to go. As for one of Reggie's big-inch engines, he wants a 0.035" - 0.040" squish band.

Installing the correct thickness head gasket creates the proper squish band. Cometic, as well as a number of other companies, make a full range of excellent gaskets in a number of thickness sizes. Here's how to know which one you need: If the top of the piston is even with the top of the cylinder at TDC, and you want a 0.035" - 0.040" squish, select a gasket that is 0.040"-thick. Since the cylinder base gasket will crush about 0.002" - 0.003" when the heads are fully torqued to spec, a 0.040" gasket, minus the 0.002" - 0.003" you're going to lose, puts you right in the middle of where you want to be: 0.037"-0.038". If the piston top is 0.003" below the cylinder deck at TDC, you may want to use a 0.035" gasket, since using a 0.040" may put you over the recommended gap. Another possibility is to mill the top of the cylinder to bring it level with the top of the piston. This eliminates the problem, as well as increases the engine's compression ratio. See the section on milling heads in this chapter for more on this option.

8: Measuring A Combustion Chamber

Before you can figure out what compression ratio your engine will have you should verify the size of the combustion chambers and that they are equal. This procedure, which is called cc'ing the heads, should be done even on a set of brand new heads, since manufacturers don't always send you a matched set.

There are two ways to do this. One is with the head on the engine, which we'll tell you how to do. The other is the much easier one and the way we're going to show you in the accompanying photos and captions. This method is done before you bolt on the heads. However, in both cases, the heads must be completely finished and ready to be installed. Any machining, lapping valves to seats, clearance checks, etc., must already be done. (You may want to put a skin coat of grease on the valve seats to make sure they don't leak for this test.) If doing the test with the heads on a bench, you also have to install the exact style and heat range spark plugs you plan on running in the engine and torque them to spec so there are no leaks. In fact, as you fill the combustion chamber with colored alcohol look into the intake and exhaust ports to make sure the alcohol is not leaking past the valves. Also check the plug. As you fill the combustion chamber you'll have to tilt the head to get rid of the air bubble under the plate.

Testing the heads when they're bolted onto the cylinders will give you the actual volume of the entire combustion chamber. This includes the head's combustion chamber and the area above the piston's rings. Start by bringing the piston in the front cylinder to the top of its compression stroke, which is also called the Top Dead Center (TDC) position. Then seal the piston rings to the cylinder with some light grease. Be sure to seal the piston all the way around the cylinder. Then install the head gasket and head onto the engine. After you remove the spark plug, tilt the engine, so the spark plug hole is the highest point of the combustion chamber. Then fill the chamber right up to the bottom thread of the spark plug hole with alcohol measured from a 100cc burette. When reading the burette, surface friction will cause the fluid to creep up the walls of the tube, making a crescent-shape, which is called a meniscus. Always read the burette's scale at the lowest part of the meniscus. Write down the number and do the same on the other cylinder.

Once you know the volume of each chamber, compare them. They must be 2cc or less of each other. If needed, you can surface (mill) the heads to get them equal. If a stock H-D Evo head must be reduced by 2cc, divide that number by the factor 142. The answer, which is 0.014", is how much material must be removed from the head's gasket surface to

<table>
<tr><td>

SPECIAL TOOL LIST

100cc burette
Set of blocks
Carpenter's level
Wheel bearing grease
1/4"-thick plastic (Plexiglas) plate 6" x 6"
Electric drill
1/4" drill bit
Countersink bit
Colored alcohol (or other thin fluid)

</td></tr>
</table>

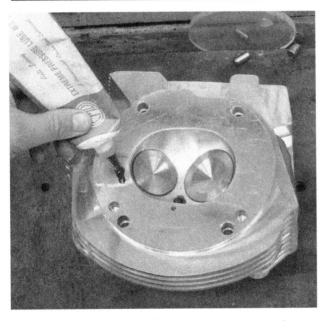

1. With the head assembled, spark plug torqued to spec, and gasket surface clean, use a carpenter's level to get the head perfectly level. Then coat the gasket surface with grease to act as a sealer. Get a 6" x 6" piece of flat 1/4"-thick Plexiglas plate and drill a 1/4" hole into the plate towards one edge.

reduce the combustion chamber volume by 2cc. As for all other brand heads, check with the manufacturer for what factor to use.

Now that you know the volume of the engine's combustion chambers, you can compute what the static compression ratio (CR) will be by adding the cylinder volume (CV) and the combustion chamber volume (CCV), and then dividing the answer you get by the combustion chamber volume (CV + CCV/CCV = CR. Here's why: the entire volume of the combustion chamber and cylinder when the piston is at the very bottom (BDC) of its intake stroke is compressed into just the volume of the combustion

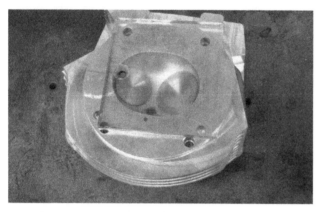

2. *After you counterbore the hole to make it easier to add alcohol, press the plastic plate onto the head and make a good complete. Do this by checking that the grease all around the head is squished down.*

3. *Carefully fill the combustion chamber with colored alcohol through the hole in the plastic plate. Once the fluid reaches the bottom of the countersunk hole, stop adding fluid and read the burette's scale.*

chamber when the piston is at the very top (TDC) of its compression stroke. This value is expressed as a ratio. A stock Evo has an 8.5:1 compression ratio.

To find out the cylinder volume, use the formula: Displacement = Bore x Bore x 0.7854 x Stroke. Using the specifications for a stock Evo engine, as listed in the service manual, the formula becomes: Displacement = 3.498" x 3.498" x 0.7854 x 4.250". The result is 40.8" per cylinder, which is half of the service manual's stated displacement of 81.6". To get this answer in cc's, just substitute the constant 0.7845 for 12.87. Or just multiply your answer of 40.8" by 16.387, which will also convert it to cc's, for a final of 669.3cc. Armed with the cylinder volume, you can now add that to the combustion chamber volume that you get after you have measured the chambers.

If you check the size of the combustion chambers with the heads off the engine, you have a couple of other dimensions to figure in before computing the compression ratio. One of these factors is the thickness of the head gasket you use, which you determined when you computed the squish. (See the previous section on this.) On a stock bore Evo, a head gasket that's 0.060"-thick when torqued to spec and compressed will add about 9.45cc of volume to the combustion chamber. A head gasket that's 0.040"-thick when torqued to spec will add 6.30cc of volume to the combustion chamber, while a 0.020" thick one adds 3.15cc of volume. Be sure to add the appropriate number to your combustion chamber figure when you do your computations.

The other factor that may affect the compression ratio is the piston dome height. In most cases, the piston will be a flat-topped one that stops even with the top of the cylinder. However, if the dome protrudes into the combustion chamber, or the dome stops below the top of the cylinder, this must also be considered when figuring the compression ratio. A quick and dirty rule of thumb for a stock H-D Evo head and flattop piston is that every 0.010" that the piston protrudes past the top of the cylinder decreases the combustion chamber volume by 1.5cc. Of course, the opposite is also true. Every 0.010" that the top of the piston is below the top of the cylinder increases the combustion chamber volume by 1.5cc. Once you figure these numbers into the combustion chamber size, you can plug the correct numbers into the compression ratio formula.

9: Milling The Heads And/Or Cylinders

There are a couple of ways to increase cylinder pressure, also known as the compression ratio, of an engine. You can install a set of pistons with pop-up domes, or mill the heads and/or cylinders. If they're going to go the milling route, many builders opt to take half the needed amount from the heads and the rest from the cylinders when a lot of material is going to be removed. However, in most cases just the heads are done, which brings up an important point. Before you mill the heads, be sure to measure the size of the combustion chamber of both heads. If there is a discrepancy, you'll need to mill the larger head down to get them to match. This will affect your computations here, so be sure to measure the combustion chambers first. Many builders also go the milling route to clean up the head's gasket surface.

Andrews Products, makers of high quality camshafts and transmission gears, has devised a formula that makes computing how much needs to be milled off a snap. This formula has been printed in its parts catalog for over a decade. The formula is: T = Stroke Length x (1/Original CR-1 – 1/New CR-1). T is the amount to mill off, while CR is compression ratio. If we want a final compression ratio of 9.5:1 and we plug in the numbers for a stock Evo 80-cubic-inch engine, which has a 4-1/4" (4.250") stroke and a stock compression ratio of 8.5:1, you get:

$$T = 4.250 \times ([1/8.5-1] - [1/9.5-1])$$
$$T = 4.250 \times (1/7.5 - 1/8.5)$$
$$T = 4.250 \times (0.133 - 0.118)$$
$$T = 4.250 \times 0.015$$
$$T = 0.064"$$

Since the maximum you should mill off each head is about 0.060", this compression increase can be done by just reworking the heads. Note: Once the heads and/or cylinders are milled, stock fixed length pushrods can't be used. I doubt you were planning on doing that, but I have to say it to cover all the bases.

By milling the heads, you've moving the piston closer to the valves. If there's not enough clearance between these parts, they will collide with the result being lots of damaged parts. The Claying The Pistons section in this chapter tells you how to check valve-to-piston and piston-to-head clearances.

To give you an idea of what compression pressures are correct for what applications, here's useful info from Andrews Products. The following are static (cranking) compression pressure ranges - what you could expect the resultant engine performance to be. Static or cranking compression is different than compression ratio. It's what the engine is producing when the starter motor is cranking the engine or it's at idle. It is dependent on compression ratio as well as the characteristics of the cam - duration, intake closing times, etc. If the engine is developing less than 115 psi static pressure, it will have poor low-speed response and be hard to start. Static pressure of 120-145 psi is a bit low for a stock street engine. 145-165 is very good for a modified street engine. Compression releases will help the starter motor do its job. Pressures in the 165-180 range are toward the upper end of what's good for a large displacement street engine - it may be hard to start, and have detonation and overheating problems. Compression releases should be used. If it's over 180 psi, I hope it's a track bike."

SPECIAL TOOL LIST
Dial indicator with flat base A shop with a milling machine

The head gasket surface on this stock H-D Evo head is what gets milled if you want to boost the engine's compression ratio without using domed pistons.

10: Claying The Pistons

There are two ways to boost your compression: milling material off the heads or/and cylinders, or using higher compression pistons. Those interested in the milling option can check out the accompanying section in this chapter to see how much has to come off to get the compression increase they want. Other people prefer to go with the piston method, since they have to upgrade to forged pistons anyway due to the increased stresses associated with higher compression ratios.

High compression (pop-up) pistons have a dome that protrudes up into the combustion chamber, instead of the flat top that the stock pistons have. The drawback of a domed piston is that the dome can get in the way of the flame front of combustion as it burns its way across the combustion chamber. However, many performance builders feel that with a moderate increase, like 9.5:1, this should not pose a problem. In fact, some piston manufacturers shape the dome so it will assist combustion by increasing the amount of turbulence in the cylinder, which results in a better mixing of the air and fuel, and, therefore, a better burn.

Either way, by mill machine or dome, you're moving the piston closer to the valves and head. The same is true if you've installed a higher lift camshaft, since this modification moves the head of the valves deeper into the combustion chamber and, therefore, closer to the piston. If there's not enough clearance between these parts, they will collide with the result being a damaged engine and bank account. The smart thing to do is always check valve-to-piston and piston-to-head clearances with modeling clay to ensure that these parts will not touch during engine operation.

This test is done after you've completely assembled the bottom end and gearcase section. The heads should be completely setup, assembled with light-duty checking springs or just the outer valve spring to ensure accurate intended valve motion, and ready to be installed. You can do the test after the pistons and cylinders are installed, but it's better to do it before in case the valve pockets in the piston domes have to be cut deeper. For the test, you can just slip the pistons onto their rods without the piston rings or wrist pin clips. Then, with the cylinder base gaskets on the crankcase, slip the cylinders over the piston.

Once the engine is setup in this way, clean the top of the piston with a solvent like brake clean. Then place a thin layer of modeling clay onto the top of the piston in both valve pockets. After you put a very thin film of oil onto the valves, install the heads complete with the head gaskets onto the cylinders. Do not torque down the head bolts (you don't want

1. With piston tops cleaned and some modeling clay in both valve pockets, use a blunt razor to trim the clay so it just fills the valve pockets. After putting a very thin film of oil onto the head of each valve, assemble the engine.

SPECIAL TOOL LIST

Modeling clay
Flat feeler gauge
Blunt razor blade
Brake clean

to stretch the cylinder studs). Just bring the bolts down until they're snug. Install the complete valve-train, but leave out the O-rings and gaskets, and just snug up the bolts. Do not torque anything. However, adjust the pushrods as if you were going to start the engine. If you don't, this test is worthless. (Don't forget to give the lifters time to bleed down.) Leave the spark plugs out.

Now that the engine is prepared in this manner, gently rotate the engine two or more full rotations by hand in the same direction it would turn if running. If you feel a hesitation, stop! However, you shouldn't unless you've done something wrong. Then remove the heads, so you can see the top of the pistons.

If you have done everything correctly, there should be an indent in some, and sometimes all, of the mounds of clay from the valves. (Hopefully, there are no places where the piston touched the head.) Carefully cut each clay section in half with a blunt razor. (Be careful not to mark the top of the piston with the razor.) First check that each valve pocket cut

into the piston is wide enough for its valve. Do this by checking where the valve cut into the clay in relation to the valve pocket. If there's not at least 0.060" of clearance between the outer edge of the valve and the inner face of the piston's pocket, have the dome of the piston machined to make it so.

Now measure the gap between the bottom of the indent in the clay and the top of the valve pocket in the piston with a flat feeler gauge. On the pistons we installed here, the indent in the clay on the intake pockets stopped 0.100" from the top of the piston. There were no marks at all in the exhaust pockets. If you're using domed pistons, follow the piston manufacturer specs regarding how much clearance they want. If the piston manufacturer does not call out a spec in its instructions, a minimum of 0.060" is the industry norm. That means we've got plenty of room with this piston, camshaft, and valve setup. If you don't have sufficient clearance, have the piston domes cut to get what you need.

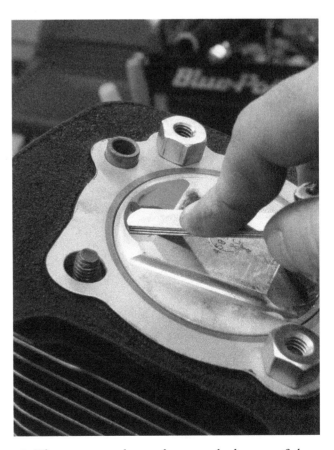

2. After gently rotating the engine two or more full rotations by hand, remove the heads. There should be an indent in some, if not all, of the clay from the valves. Carefully cut each clay section in half with a blunt razor.

3. Then measure the gap between the bottom of the indent and the top of the piston with a flat feeler gauge.

11: Heat Cycles & Break-In

There are many different theories on what a new engine needs in terms of break-in. The way I see it, if you push the engine too soon, you could damage it and end up redoing part or all of your work. And contrary to what I've seen people do, the engine doesn't heal itself if you then ride it nice for a while. It's not like pulling a muscle. Once a component or components (which is usually the case), is/are damaged they will only get worse, not better, the more you use the engine.

I prefer to follow a conservative break-in procedure. This way, the worst that can happen is I have to wait a while before I can play. I can't possibly hurt the engine by taking it easy for the early stages of its, hopefully, long service life. Once the beast has 1,000 miles or so on it, all I have to watch out for is making a stupid mistake while using it, such as staying on the throttle when the engine is pinging.

The most critical time for an engine is how it's treated during the first couple of hours of its life. In fact, the first hour is the most dangerous. A common mistake is to spend a lot of time admiring the new addition as it sits there idling. And overheating! When the engine is brand new is when it's most prone to overheating. The mating surface of new parts is actually rough, relatively speaking, which causes a lot of friction, resulting in excessive heat buildup. The main purpose of breaking in an engine is to give the moving parts time to wear in to each other and smooth out the rough spots. How much time they need depends on how tight the engine has been built.

A tight engine has the clearances between its moving parts towards the tighter end of their tolerance ranges. For example, if a part has a fit tolerance of 0.001" - 0.008", the tight clearance would be 0.001" - 0.003". A tight engine is also more susceptible to damage from overheating, a heavy throttle hand, or poor lubrication issues, such as insufficient or dirty oil. As the engine's components wear in (seat), the level of friction drops, which also reduces the heat that the engine generates. Overheating an engine, especially

> **SPECIAL TOOL LIST**
> _____
>
> Three oil filters
> Seven tanks of gas
> 12 quarts of oil
> Lots of patience

When an engine is overheated or not properly broken in, the victim is usually a piston or two. This one came out of a new engine that got too hot and was revved too high during the initial break-in. Pretty, isn't it?

a new one, can result in piston, cylinder, and other internal component damage. And piston damage is the most common reason why an engine is torn down for rebuilding.

Since an Evo is an air-cooled engine, it needs air passing through the head and cylinder cooling fins to maintain its proper operating temperature. That's why you shouldn't let it idle at a standstill longer than necessary. If you have to make fuel, ignition, or any other adjustments before getting on the road, have a large fan blowing air onto the engine to keep it cool while you're spinning wrenches.

While breaking in a new motor, there are a few things you should avoid, all of which have to do with heat and rpm. Extended periods with the engine idling, riding in stop-and-go traffic, carrying a passenger, or pulling a heavy load, like towing a trailer or a sidecar, can cause engine damage due to excessive heat buildup.

And while we'll get to what the rpm limits are for different stages of the break-in period in a minute, lugging a motor should also be avoided. Lugging an engine, which is letting its revs drop too low when under a load, can also cause severe engine damage. The touring guys are the biggest offenders here. Looking to keep their revs down to get as many miles as possible from a gallon of gas, they make their motor struggle to pull a full bagger, usually loaded down with a ton of gear, as well as two riders. Damage to the pistons and rings, as well as from pinging/engine knock, is possible, especially in hot weather. Keeping the revs between 2500-3000 rpm (except during the

I prefer to follow a conservative break-in procedure. This way, the worst that can happen is I have to wait a while before I can play.

first 50 miles when it should not go above 2500) when on the throttle, as well as always running 91-octane or higher fuel, will help prevent pinging/knock. However, if it does occur, downshift to bring the engine's revs up. Never try to power your way through a pinging/knock condition with more throttle. If a mental picture will help, think of every ping as a hammer hitting the top of the piston, since that's close to what's happening to it inside your engine.

I suggest you follow the advice of noted high performance engine shop R&R Cycle when it comes to heat cycles and rpm limits during the different stages of break-in. According to R&R's recommended break-in procedure, when the moment of truth has finally arrived, start the engine using its normal procedure. Once it fires off, you should only let the engine run for about a minute at 1250 - 1750 rpm, which is a fast idle. Resist the urge, no matter how strong it is, to crack the throttle, since the head gaskets are very susceptible to failure at this stage. While the engine is running, make sure the oil pressure is normal, there are no leaks, and that oil is returning to the oil tank. Then shut down the engine and, while you give it a good going over, looking for leaks or other problems, let the engine get cool to the touch.

Start the motor back up and allow it to get hotter this time. You can let it run three to four minutes, or until the cylinders become warm/hot to the touch, whichever happens first. During this time make sure you have oil pressure, etc. Then shut the motor down and again let it cool to the ambient temperature. While it's cooling off, do the same stuff you did the first time: Look for leaks, etc.

You should repeat this procedure three or four times. Each time you fire it off the engine should take slightly longer to warm up. You can also let the motor get slightly hotter each time. In the final run, gently vary the rpm continuously from idle up to 2500. Don't blip the throttle. Don't be too concerned with the final carb settings at this time (if you're running one), since the idle speed and mixture can't be properly set until the motor reaches full operating temperature, which is what it shouldn't do during these preliminary runs. After letting the motor cool down after the final run, you're ready to start the 1,000-mile engine break-in procedure.

The first 50 miles are the most critical ones for the rings and pistons, so avoid conditions that can cause overheating. Do not exceed 3500 rpm, or, if you don't have a tach, stay under 50-55 mph on the highway in fifth gear during this time. You can now set the idle speed and mixture, as well as change the other fuel settings, but only do so if the engine is not running properly, especially if it's too lean. Do not do power runs to dial the fuel settings in. Also, don't keep the engine turning at a steady speed; vary its rpm and don't lug it. Basically, ride it around town, shifting often and staying out of traffic. Be sure to take it easy with the throttle and keep the load that the engine has to pull to a minimum, which means definitely no trailers, sidecars, or passengers. After the first 50 miles, change the oil and filter. Also

keep the engine clean, so you can quickly see if there are any fuel, oil, or exhaust leaks.

During the next 500 miles, you can bring the revs up to 4000 rpm (about 60 mph), which is above the normal shift point for most people, for short periods of time. Continue to vary the engine's rpm, while avoiding overheating, lugging, and staying at a steady speed. Once these 500 miles are done, change the oil and filter again.

Now that you've got 550 miles on the motor, you can be a little more aggressive with the throttle during the next 450 miles. You can run the engine in a normal, but conservative manner. However, that doesn't mean you can whack the throttle wide open or go drag racing; nor should you haul any heavy loads. Continue to vary the engine's rpm, while avoiding overheating or lugging the motor. Definitely do some around town riding, which gives you plenty of opportunities to go through the gears, bringing the engine up and down its rpm range. Definitely take long rides on the highway but keep within the 2500 – 3000 rpm range with short bursts at higher rpm.

Once you've got over 1,000 miles on it, you can finally have some fun -- the engine is now fully broken-in. Dial in the carb's jetting/EFI settings and change the oil and filter again. If you want to load the beast up, pull a trailer, or rip through the gears, have at it. However, overheating, lugging, and pinging/engine knock should always to be avoided.

That is, unless you had so much fun building it the first time you can't wait to do it again.

The most critical time for an engine is how it's treated during the first couple of hours of its life. In fact, the first hour is the most dangerous.

Books from Wolfgang Publications can be found at many book stores and numerous web sites.

Titles	ISBN	Price	# of pages
Advanced Airbrush Art	9781929133208	$29.95	144 pages
Advanced Custom Motorcycle Assembly & Fabrication	9781929133239	$29.95	144 pages
Advanced Custom Motorcycle Wiring - *Revised*	9781935828761	$29.95	144 pages
Advanced Pinstripe Art	9781929133321	$29.95	144 pages
Advanced Sheet Metal Fab	9781929133123	$29.95	144 pages
Advanced Tattoo Art - *Revised*	9781929133822	$29.95	144 pages
Airbrush How-To with Mickey Harris	9781929133505	$29.95	144 pages
Building Hot Rods	9781929133437	$29.95	144 pages
Colorful World of Tattoo Models	9781935828716	$34.95	144 pages
Composite Materials 1	9781929133765	$29.95	144 pages
Composite Materials 2	9781929133932	$29.95	144 pages
Composite Materials 3	9781935828662	$29.95	144 pages
Composite Materials Step by Step Projects	9781929133369	$29.95	144 pages
Cultura Tattoo Sketchbook	9781935828839	$32.95	284 pages
Custom Bike Building Basics	9781935828624	$24.95	144 pages
Custom Motorcycle Fabrication	9781935828792	$29.95	144 pages
Harley-Davidson Sportster Hop-Up & Customizing Guide	9781935828952	$29.95	144 pages
Harley-Davidson Sportser Buell Engine Hop-Up Guide	9781929133093	$27.95	144 pages
Harley-Davidson Twin Cam-Hop Up	9781929133697	$29.95	144 pages
Harley-Davidson Evo Hop-Up/Build	9781941064337	$29.95	144 pages
How Airbrushes Work	9781929133710	$24.95	144 pages
Honda Enthusiast Guide Motorcycles 1959-1985	9781935828853	$29.95	144 pages
Honda Mini Trail	9781941064320	$29.95	144 pages
How-To Airbrush, Pinstripe & Goldleaf	9781935828693	$29.95	144 pages
How-To Build Old Skool Bobber - 2nd Edition	9781935828785	$29.95	144 pages

Books from Wolfgang Publications can be found at many book stores and numerous web sites.

Titles	ISBN	Price	# of pages
How-To Build a Cheap Chopper	9781929133178	$29.95	144 pages
How-To Build Cafe Racer	9781935828730	$29.95	144 pages
How-To Chop Tops	9781929133499	$24.95	144 pages
How-To Fix American V-Twin	9781929133727	$29.95	144 pages
How-To Paint Tractors & Trucks	9781929133475	$29.95	144 pages
Hot Rod Wiring	9781929133987	$29.95	144 pages
Hot Rod Chassis How-To	9781929133703	$29.95	144 Pages
Kosmoski's *New* Kustom Paint Secrets	9781929133833	$29.95	144 pages
Learning the English Wheel	9781935828891	$29.95	144 pages
Mini Ebooks - Butterfly and Roses	9781935828167	Ebook Only	
Mini Ebooks - Skulls & Hearts	9781935828198	Ebook Only	
Mini Ebooks - Lettering & Banners	9781935828204	Ebook Only	
Mini Ebooks - Tribal Stars	9781935828211	Ebook Only	
Power Hammers	9781929133604	$29.95	144 pages
Pro Pinstripe	9781929133925	$29.95	144 pages
Sheet Metal Bible	9781929133901	$29.95	176 pages
Sheet Metal Fab Basics B&W	9781929133468	$24.95	144 pages
Sheet Metal Fab for Car Builders	9781929133383	$29.95	144 pages
SO-CAL Speed Shop, Hot Rod Chassis	9781935828860	$29.95	144 pages
Tattoo Bible #1	9781929133840	$29.95	144 pages
Tattoo Bible #2	9781929133857	$29.95	144 pages
Tattoo Bible #3	9781935828754	$29.95	144 pages
Tattoo Lettering Bible	9781935828921	$29.95	144 pages
Tattoo Sketchbook, Jim Watson	9781935828037	$32.95	112 pages
Triumph Restoration - Pre Unit	9781929133635	$29.95	144 pages
Triumph Restoration - Unit 650cc	9781929133420	$29.95	144 pages
Vintage Dirt Bikes - Enthusiast's Guide	9781929133314	$29.95	144 pages
Ultimate Sheet Metal Fab	9780964135895	$24.95	144 pages
Ultimate Triumph Collection	9781935828655	$49.95	144 pages

 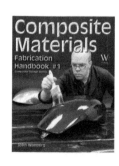   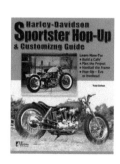